THE UNREAL GOD OF
MODERN THEOLOGY

THE
UNREAL GOD
OF
MODERN THEOLOGY

Bultmann, Barth, and the
theology of atheism:
a call to recovering
the truth of God's reality

KLAUS BOCKMUEHL

Translated by
Geoffrey W. Bromiley

HELMERS & HOWARD
COLORADO SPRINGS

English translation © 1988 by Klaus Bockmuehl.

Translated from the German *Atheismus in der Christenheit. Die Unwirklichkeit Gottes in Theologie und Kirche*, 3rd ed. (Giessen and Basel: Brunnen-Verlag, 1985).

Published by Helmers & Howard, Publishers, Inc., P.O. Box 7407, Colorado Springs, CO 80933 USA.

Library of Congress Cataloging-in-Publication Data

Bockmühl, Klaus.
    The unreal God of modern theology : Bultmann, Barth, and
    the theology of atheism : a call to recovering the truth of
    God's reality / Klaus Bockmuehl.
          p.   cm.
    Bibliography: p.
    Includes index.
    ISBN 0-939443-11-2
    1. Theology, Doctrinal—History—20th century.   2. God.
    3. Atheism—History—20th century.   4. Bultmann, Rudolf
    Karl, 1884-1976.   5. Barth, Karl, 1886-1968.   I. Title.
    BT28.B617 1988
    231'.09'04—dc19   88-24679
                                                      CIP

Printed in the United States of America.

CONTENTS

THE UNREAL GOD OF
MODERN THEOLOGY

INTRODUCTION

NOT LONG AGO, I attended a church in the eastern half of Canada. The preacher also was a visitor, and a professor of theology. He took as his text Psalm 96 ("Oh, sing to the Lord a new song") and read to us all those predications: "Proclaim the good news of his salvation . . . his glory . . . his wondrous works among all peoples. . . . Say among the nations, The Lord reigns . . . For he is coming, for he is coming to judge the earth," etc. He then went on to elaborate that we today did not, of course, experience the strength, beauty, holiness, wonders, and mighty deeds of God. But we were invited, he said, in spite of the absence of God in our lives, to "enjoy God as who he truly is *in and for himself.*" The preacher recommended this attitude of "objective" faith over against the "unhealthy self-concern" of other forms of religion that spoke of an experience of God; they were indeed idolatrous in that they attempted to make God tangible. We were meant to believe, not to see.

I was rather upset at this kind of interpretation of Psalm 96, and after the service engaged in a lively discussion with friends at that church. They praised the sermon as "one of

1

the best ever." I tried to point out that the psalm itself culminated in the twofold assertion that God would *come* and not stay in the distance of being "in and for himself," and that he had since actually come for our sake in the person of Christ—of which the sermon had not made a single reference—and was still coming to us in the person of the Holy Spirit. My friends, however, felt that they did not have the psalmist's "unproblematic confidence" in God. They did not experience God's mighty works, and the preacher's description of the human predicament was "very much where they lived." Thus it was a relief for them and the solution to an apparent dilemma: to be able to believe in God with all his riches even though he existed in the distant beyond. I went away with the impression that the preacher had provided them with a suitable theory to vindicate a practical state of affairs which seemed to me profoundly disturbing: the state, as it were, of a nominal Christianity which is a late stage of religion on the road to secularization.

I was also made aware that this sermon was but an extension, the tip of an iceberg, of a vast school of theological opinion, dominant for the past fifty years or so, which had consistently removed the things of God from the reality of time and space in which we live. Two of the most influential theologians of the century, Rudolf Bultmann and Karl Barth (in his earlier years), among others, heavily taught to this effect. Here they pursued a common goal, whatever considerable differences they otherwise may have had. They evacuated God from the danger zone of philosophical debate, perhaps not so much in order to adapt theology to the practical reality of the people in the pew, but to comply with the theoretical, so-called scientific demands of a modern secular world view which allows no room for divine interference in this world. The result was the sweeping rule in theology of a philosophical cast centred in the unreality of God—a factual, if not a nominal, atheism.

The more pressing recent socio-theological issue concerning the relation of Christian theology to revolutionary ideologies cannot be understood apart from these basic presuppositions of the theological mind in the twentieth century that were worked out in the generation of Barth and Bultmann. The connection is startling and compelling. A whole development, sometimes by way of a conscious inversion, can be traced from the theologies of Barth and Bultmann to the later proposals for an "atheistic Christianity" or "Christian atheism" and their concurrent political programs.

One of the great heterodox Marxists of this century, Ernst Bloch, who had the ear of a whole generation of restless students, has suggested that once the idea of a kingdom of God was removed from it, Christianity was quite a useful thing; he concluded that only an atheist could be a good Christian, and only a Christian could be a good atheist. He gave his respective book the intriguing title, *Atheism in Christianity*. Bloch was wide off the mark. But he would indeed have been correct had he said that there was atheism in Christendom, in the church, and, not least, in its theology.

It is this kind of virtual atheism—what one could call the dimming of the doctrine of God—that this book will deal with. It will investigate the important sectors of modern theology that, in an act of self-censorship, have succumbed to secularism, falling in line with the ideological demands and valuations of the contemporary mindset. Throughout the following discussion, I understand atheism therefore to be that thought and action which leaves no place for the reality of God, and perhaps no room for his personality and dominion either. The overriding questions at every point—and not just in the extremes of the so-called Death-of-God theology—are: Is God the *living* God? Does he show himself as living? Is he active and real? The questions we must raise throughout are the questions of God's reality or unreality, his activity or inactivity, his presence or absence in the world and above all in man.

As we study some of the dominant systems of theology of

our time, trying to find out what they teach about God, we
begin with the conviction that theology must always be
partisan. This does not at all mean that one has to join a
theological, ideological, or denominational "camp" in order
to gain a footing. On the other hand, the refusal to commit
oneself to a specific theological party—to praise its tenets
and condemn all others—but instead attempt to distinguish what is good and bad in a given theology, does not
mean pure and simple neutrality. Neutrality is in itself a
choice. Indeed, all theology necessitates a commitment.

At the very outset, therefore, we must make clear that the
present study does make certain presuppositions. Christian theology cannot but do so. It begins with a basic
assumption to which it is committed at every point. Its
commitment lies in its basis and its goal: that is, in the
promise and the program: "Your will be done, on earth as it
is in heaven" (Matt. 6:10). If it is true to its essence,
Christian theology will serve the hope of a large-scale swing
back to the will of God—in theology, church, and culture.
Once we have arrived at the end of our investigation, it will
be clear that nothing less than this is needed.

If this is the horizon and measure of theology, the battle
line cuts right across the positions of the traditional parties
organized in the church. Solidarity with this or that theological trend is not the same as turning to the will of God. A
commitment to a particular school or theological standpoint can actually obscure the need for a return to life and
work under the prayer Jesus gave. This is something of
which we need to be constantly aware.

Once we follow a particular line, it is inevitable that we
will be led into debate, criticism, and polemics. Some
people are asking today whether there is any place at all for
criticism in church and theology. A few put the question so
earnestly that words fail them forthwith. Does not the
gospel forbid judging? On the other hand, we are also told
to bring to light and to censure "the unprofitable works of

darkness." How are we to reconcile the two? To judge means to liquidate the opponent. It means a diagnosis followed by outright rejection and abandonment of the patient, with no hope for recovery. But abandoning a person is the self-righteousness that is impermissible. It is wrong to think that conservatives—or liberals—in the church are beyond hope. No one is beyond hope; and over time, one can hear unexpected statements from different quarters of the church that come as both negative and positive surprises. On the other hand, we would be misconstruing the saying of Jesus if we found in it a command against factual observation or objective thought.

We are dealing here not with personal conduct but with public teaching. We must be absolutely clear and unequivocal with this distinction between the person and the teaching. We must respect unconditionally the people whose views we critically analyze and respect their achievements on a human level. At the same time, we must oppose the mistaken theological view they have championed, in the hope that we may come to future agreement. In his dealings with schismatic bishops, St. Augustine followed this rule: Honor the person, fight the error. He laid down the polemical principle that we must contend objectively with reasons and with proofs from Holy Scripture, and with the desire to win a person back, as he succeeded in doing in at least one instance. His motto was: *Diligite homines, interficite errores;* Love the people, and destroy the errors.

This perspective is necessary because no one can see into a person's heart. It is not for us to judge anyone as such. But the Christian community certainly has the privilege and task to evaluate what is being taught. Again, we may find both good and bad in someone's teaching. But we cannot play off one against the other; we cannot ignore the bad because of the good. It would be the same as excusing a pharmaceutical firm for a dangerous medicine because of the excellent penicillin preparations it has produced for

years. It may go on producing excellent medicine, but
production of the dangerous substance must be censured
and stopped as well as restitution made.

In relation to opinions rather than people, teachings
rather than teachers, we thus agree with Martin Luther
when he wrote that the devil has his schemes for Christian
schools through which "he worms his way into Holy Scripture. When he has gained entry and is sure of things he then
lashes out on all sides, brings rubbish into Scripture and
sets up many sects and heresies and groups among Christians. . . . He then goes on attacking more articles, as he is
already flashing his eyes that baptism, original sin and
Christ are nothing. . . . Nor do we see how peace can be
expected from him; he takes no time off and does not sleep.
So, decide whether you would rather tussle with the devil or
be one of his. If you want to be one of his, he will give you a
safe-conduct and will let you be at peace with Scripture. If
you do not, be on guard, catch him by the hair as he will
certainly do to you. . . ."

This kind of warfare is not abnormal for the church. We
can view its progress in human history as a long march.
Like Israel in its forty years in the wilderness, the community of God is en route. The old die, infants are born,
strangers join in, and the embattled march goes on. We may
think of the column as accompanied by all sorts of people
with megaphones who march alongside and make recom-
mendations, offer proposals, suggest corrections of the
route, all of course in the best interest of the marchers and
certainly in terms they can understand. Sometimes, one of
the marchers themselves will seize a megaphone and advo-
cate a deviation. In any case, these incidents must be dealt
with according to the Arab proverb: The dogs bark, but the
caravan moves on. The church, however, will never be
without the barking and biting.

Debate is good, even necessary, for Christianity. We
might even say that the people of God stand in need of false

teachers and prophets. "When a prophet arises and calls upon you to go after idols," says Moses in Deuteronomy, "you must not follow him, for *God is testing you* in order to learn whether you love him with all your heart and with all your soul. You must follow the Lord your God and fear him and keep his commandments and obey his voice and serve him and cleave to him" (Deut. 13:1ff.) There is a criterion here regarding the voices that press upon us. If they attempt to bring us to obey God's voice and to love him with all our hearts and keep his commandments, they are good, no matter what language or dialect they speak.

But other voices also have a part to play. We have to be tested in order to be proved. For as Luther says, "If there were no sects through whom the devil rouses us, we should be lazy, we should sleep and snore to death; both faith and the Word would be obscured and resisted until all was lost. But, sects rub and polish us. They grind our faith and teaching so that these are smooth and pure and shine like a mirror. . . . Moreover, the Word itself is also set before the world far better and more clearly thereby, so that through this conflict many learn the truth and are strengthened therein."

1

DISMANTLING THE TRUTH:
Bultmann's Program of Demythologization

THE PROGRAM OF RUDOLF BULTMANN

CONTEMPORARY THEOLOGICAL DEBATE HAS an important point of departure in the publication of Rudolf Bultmann's *The New Testament and Mythology.* Appearing in 1941, this essay first began to exert great influence only ten years later but then began to quickly dominate the scene. In his work, the Marburg theologian elaborated the conditions of intellectual life in the age of science and technology, and demanded that the New Testament be demythologized in order to make the gospel accessible to the abilities of modern understanding. This seminal work, more than any other, articulated the platform upon which modern theology has been built.

The epistemological question: *"this world" vs. "the beyond"*

In *The New Testament and Mythology,* Bultmann sets out from the fact that the whole orientation of modern thought has been determined by the Enlightenment's epistemological critique.

Theology and the interpretation of the New Testament must operate within this framework. In his *Critique of Pure Reason,* Kant investigated the possibilities of natural theology and metaphysics: Can man secure a definitive concept of God by reason alone apart from revelation? Through criticism, e.g. of the traditional proofs for the existence of God, he concluded that human understanding cannot say anything cogent and universally valid about that which is beyond the sense world. An impenetrable cover lies over the world. Even if thought can get beyond this, it can do so only by means of theory and logical deduction. Real existence, however, could not be ascribed to a deduced concept of God, not even to God as a necessary being. No one could prove the existence of an absolute being or of God. On the other hand, neither could one disprove it. Reason alone is inadequate either way.

One result of Kant's critique is a sharp division of the world into "this side" and "the beyond." These concepts will be significant in all that follows. On this side, in nature and history, specific laws hold. (These may be summed up in the two principles of causality and analogy. Each event has an immanent cause and immanent results. Each event is analogous to other immanent events.) About the beyond, nothing can be said for certain. The wall that separates this world and the beyond is impenetrable.[1] No intervention of the beyond into this world, such as God's revelation of himself in history, can take place.[2] No Messiah can ever come, on principle.

The division of the world into this side (which is under iron laws we can largely know and control) and the beyond (about which nothing can be said or known) plays a dominant role in modernity and assigns a specific place, or no place at all, to metaphysics and theology.

For the sake of Christian proclamation, modern theology must come to terms with these presuppositions. In his demythologization program, Bultmann makes the division of this side and the beyond his starting point. To begin with, the conflict between "the mythical world view of the Bible" and the world view fashioned by scientific thought makes demythologization necessary.[3] But not this world view alone, for Bultmann goes on to distinguish between the world view of modern science and the "self-understanding of modern man." Man is born into the former as into his age; he cannot change it. The latter, however, Bultmann describes as an object of human decision. Man decides for it; it does not come upon him of necessity. It is this self-understanding that is the source of the "more serious challenge" of statements in the Bible.[4] Bultmann describes the two main forms of the modern self-understanding: *idealism,* in which man sees himself as wholly spirit; and *naturalism,* in which he sees himself as wholly nature. Variations between the two may be adopted. But, for present purposes, says Bultmann, the two main forms, though at opposite poles, are one. In both views modern man sees himself as a unitary being—a self-enclosed, inner unity not open to intervention by supernatural powers. In his worldly activity, therefore, man realizes that he is independent and solely responsible for his control of nature since both he and nature are on *this side.*[5] The closed character of the universe in Kant's cosmology now becomes the closed character of man's existence in terms of an existentialist anthropology.

This unitary, self-enclosed nature of man also takes on ethical significance. The criticism of the form and content of the gospel by the self-understanding of modern man is well brought out by C. Hartlich and W. Sachs in a hefty summary which Bultmann himself has endorsed: "The mythological is what cannot really happen since: (1) It *cannot* be established by the general rules of science (miracles are *impossible*), (2) it conflicts with the conditions of the unity of personal life (God's medium is only the spirit in the sense of 'the intelligible'; the non-spiritual cannot communicate divine things), (3) it contradicts moral axioms (to ascribe

lesser morality to God is to demonize Him), (4) it lacks
saving significance relevant for the personal life of the
individual (existentially irrelevant events are hopeless)."[6]

The presuppositions implied by "cannot" and "impossible" are applied as a critical norm to the apostolic message.
As a result, stories of the Ascension and the Descent into
Hell, the New Testament miracles, and mythical eschatology are to be excised as outdated. (Mythical eschatology
supposedly is disproved by the simple fact that Christ's
parousia did not take place as expected; but world history
has continued and by every reckoning will still continue.)[7]
The "self-understanding" of man will lead to further judgments of this kind.

Conflicting claims: the Bible
and the modern world view

We see, then, that the modern world view is a kind of
narrow gate. The Bible and the modern world view in their
respective ways both claim validity in the objective world,
the world of objects. All mythology—that of the New
Testament as well as that of Greece—objectifies; it trans-
poses the other world, the beyond, into this world. Myths
are statements of religious proclamation which speak of the
intervention of the beyond into this world, crossing the
boundary, in order to give to other-worldly reality an
objectivity in the time and space of this world. This leads to
a hopeless conflict between the objective claims of modern
self-understanding and the objective claims of myth. In the
battle between the objectifying thought of myth and the
objectifying thought of science, the latter is naturally the
victor.[8] But what place remains for the objectivity of the
gospel? If modern man cannot be expected to accept the
New Testament world view, why should he think the *proclamation* of the New Testament—the *kerygma*—has some
independent validity?[9]

Bultmann holds that the modern world view is incontestable. Yet the proclamation of the New Testament, in his view, must also maintain its validity.[10] The latter is what has been called his church or missionary concern.

For Bultmann this poses a dilemma to which only one solution is possible. If New Testament proclamation is to maintain its validity, it must be demythologized.

The solution: demythologization

This is the first argument for Bultmann's program of demythologization: Faith must let go of the world of objectivity. Demythologization must deobjectify the New Testament message.

There is a second argument for demythologization. Myths themselves, says Bultmann, do not pretend to be cosmological statements; they are anthropological statements. They do not speak of the world, but of man. Myths employ the objects of time and space to say something about the nature and experience of man. The truth of myth is in the realm of anthropology. Demythologization or deobjectification, which is made necessary by the modern world view, is also necessary as a fulfillment of the aim of myth to speak about human existence.[11] Negatively, demythologization is deobjectification; positively, it is existential interpretation.

What has all this to do with the New Testament? Bultmann's answer is that the New Testament, too, because it contains a good deal of myth, presents the beyond in terms of this world. It also shares the secret aim of myth: to make statements about human existence. Indeed, the New Testament itself, according to Bultmann, takes the first step toward demythologization. We find myths alongside direct statements on human existence.

Thus, one statement often contradicts another. These contradictions, which render the New Testament largely inaccessible to modern readers, can be resolved only by consistent demythologization along the lines already indicated by the New Testament. This is how one can deal with the contradictions—e.g. between determinism and free decision, the indicative and the imperative, or the objective promise of salvation and the demand for action with a view to salvation. In these antitheses Bultmann sees two different views of man: namely, as a cosmic being on the one side and an autonomous "I" on the other. Henceforth, exposition of the New Testament must proceed according to the attempts of speaking in terms of the self-understanding of man that are perceivable in the New Testament itself. Thus for Bultmann it is not the objectifications of myth that are to be studied, but the understanding of existence expressed by them. This is the truth that faith affirms; it is not committed to the conceptual world of the New Testament.[12]

Bultmann's program, then, is clear: the demythologization and the existential interpretation of the New Testament. He discusses his program and the difficulties that it may encounter making use of the New Testament antithesis between the old and the new man. What the New Testament says about man's inauthentic modes of existence, his life under the dominion of sin—the old man—as well as what it says about the existence of the believer—the new man—may be completely demythologized and rendered in secular terms. But the transition, the leap from one to the other, the liberation of man from himself for authentic life—can this be expressed in terms of philosophy? Can it be understood except as an act of God? According to Bultmann himself, what distinguishes the New Testament from philosophy, and faith from natural self-understanding, is this speech of an act of God which first makes possible man's authentic life.[13]

Can this so-called act of God (still mythological language!) finally be demythologized, deobjectified and interpreted existentially? Bultmann thinks not. Philosophy has no place for it. One can describe the transition but can not thereby actualize it. Philosophy thinks knowledge means control of human existence as man's own possibility, but this is a sign of the fall. It must be made plain that the new being is a gift; man does not possess it. Though other philosophers also speak of "being" as a gift, for Bultmann this is just a rudiment of the Christian view. The character of "being" as a gift is not learned from "being" itself. The new life must be granted to man from outside. *This importation is the special feature of the gospel.* It takes place in man's encounter with proclamation. As the Word goes forth, the cross and resurrection become present. The risen Lord is encountered in the preached Word and in it alone.[14] Only the "That" of his coming should be proclaimed;[15] the details of the traditional message of the historical Jesus are unimportant. And the message is not strictly one of something imparted; it is meant to trigger something in the hearer, a new self-understanding, which sees his own existence as a gift. But this message or stimulus does not lie in human life itself; it must come from outside.

This finding brings to light a basic dilemma of demythologization. Its postulate was to interpret the gospel in such a way that it does not impinge on the objectifying thought of modern man at all. But if demythologization were completely successful in this regard, proclamation would be superfluous. The gospel could say nothing that man cannot already tell himself. Bultmann, however, cannot accept this inference, for the gospel must maintain its validity. What then? Does a mythological remnant remain? He replies that one can call "God's action" mythology if one likes, but it is no longer mythology in the old sense, and salvation is not a miraculous or supernatural event.[16]

Thus mythology is no longer objectifying speech. The historical event (the cross and resurrection understood objectively) has been reinterpreted as an eschatological event, and as such it is both *in* time and *beyond* time. We do not look back to a past event, but to its significance which is always present for faith.[17]

This is Bultmann's distinctive position between biblical proclamation and modern self-understanding. Thus he describes the place where God's act occurs in time and space *but in such a way that this event never collides with the things of this world.* Time, space, place, and history do not have here the same meaning as in objective life; rather, they denote a reality beyond it.

At the end of *The New Testament and Mythology,* Bultmann distinguishes his teaching from myth by saying that God's transcendence is not made immanent as in myth. His claim is that he maintains the paradox of the presence of the transcendent God in history: The Word was made flesh.[18] This distinction between his teaching and myth points to a distinction of the locale of revelation. For myth, God comes into this world; for Bultmann, he comes into "history" (*Geschichte*). More accurately, he does not *come;* he permanently *is.* But are this world and history different? For Bultmann, they are. He has no objection, for example, to speaking liturgically of a "history" of God with man so long as interpretation divests the expression of its mythological, objectifying sense. It is essential to note that for Bultmann, "history" here does not have the same meaning as when we speak, say, of the history of Anglo-German relations.[19] The transcendent enters the immanent in a quite different manner.[20] "History" here means a constant present, a *timeless* process which simply had its origin in the historical event of the cross of Jesus Christ. Christ's cross and passion are present, not to be restricted to the past event. J. Schniewind comments that while Bultmann lays great stress on the historical significance of the cross, what he has in view is not the historical particularity of the revelation of God but "historicity" (*Geschichtlichkeit*), or rather, relevance, as a form of human life-fulfillment.[22]

What we see here, then, is an attempt to find and describe

as God's saving work a reality which has nothing at all to do with the reality of the world and which therefore cannot be in conflict with it.

CRITICAL CONSIDERATIONS

A comprehensive exposition of the program of demytholog-ization is not possible here, and so neither is a comprehen-sive criticism. But three points deserve critical attention. The first is Bultmann's obvious attachment to what he calls the modern self-understanding. The second arises from the method of demythologizing which either does not achieve its end or brings us to something that cannot be distin-guished from atheism. The third is the loss of reality which theology and proclamation suffer when subjected to alien philosophical concepts.

The self-understanding of modern man: an alien norm for theology

Attention and surprise are awakened by Bultmann's thesis that the modern scientific and technological world view and, even more, the self-understanding of modern man must be adopted as the self-evident starting point for a discussion of the future proclamation of the gospel. We have already noted Bultmann's distinction between modern world view and modern self-understanding. Bultmann says that we are born into the modern view as into our age, so that we have no choice in the matter; only the labor of generations can change a world view. The self-understand-ing of modern man, however, is a matter of individual decision and does not have the same character of ineluc-tability. Indeed, there are many different forms of this self-understanding. Dependence on a decision, too, means that we are dealing not with so-called natural laws, but, as in everything affecting the sphere of culture and society, with evaluations and postulations. Bultmann himself offers as an example of this self-understanding the enhanced significance given to the concept of race or people in 1941—obviously an evaluation.

The distinction between world view and self-understanding is a strange one. Even stranger is the thesis that a chosen self-understanding should be the main criterion in criticizing the traditional form of the gospel, for in the area of self-understanding everything is in a constant state of change. How can any passing opinion of this kind be recognized as a criterion for criticism of the gospel? Will it not become quickly outdated?[23]

It is also questionable whether the modern scientific and technological view of the world indeed makes Bultmann's program necessary. Some scientists (cf. the works of A. Loen and C. F. von Weizsäcker) have reached conclusions very different from Bultmann's assumptions. It may well be the case sometime soon that the modern scientific view of the world has nothing to say in opposition to the New Testament message, since the New Testament is not making cosmological statements that give rise to controversy.

On the other hand, if the modern self-understanding *is* made a critical criterion, this clearly involves the introduction of what is often called ideology or *Weltanschauung*. Bultmann himself regards these terms as synonymous with "self-understanding."[24] But systems of this kind are decidedly evaluations, and it is hard to see how a conflict between such self-understandings and the evaluations of the New Testament can be avoided. The gospel itself presupposes that false value-systems exist which will destroy man even if he thinks he has come of age and evaluates his particular system as factual and objectively correct.

Nor does it help to answer, as Bultmann does, that though different self-understandings—naturalism, say, or idealism—disagree in some respects, they agree at least in their

belief that human existence is closed to supernatural inter-
ventions. For this, too, is a value judgment. C. F. von
Weizsäcker, the noted German physicist, tells the story of a
prominent scientist of the older generation whose mind had
been formed by the attitudes of the nineteenth century, and
who used to become quite angry if anyone talked to him
about the "age" of the world. His emotion showed that the
eternity of the world was, for him, much more than a
hypothesis which, in the light of better knowledge, might
be dispassionately abandoned. His conviction that the
world had no beginning was not a conclusion based on
scientific observation but a personal and subjective decision. In this eminent scientist's reaction, von Weizsäcker
saw the deeply irrational element of faith in science. For him
the world had replaced God and it was blasphemy to deny it
divine attributes.[25]

No less instructive is the establishment of the thesis that
the world has no beginning, based on a passionate criticism
of the concept of creation, in the work of Karl Marx, another
leading light of the nineteenth century. If the world had a
beginning, he reasoned rightly, it had to have a creator. If it
had a creator, it had a lord, both now and always. But this
was irreconcilable with his promethean concept of human
autonomy which, with its implied value judgments, he
personally chose as the basis of self-understanding. Therefore, there must not be a creator.[26]

It is interesting to see that for Bultmann, too, the infinity
and endless duration of the world are among the theses of
the modern self-understanding with which the Christian
faith must not collide. That the world has no beginning now
seems to be an idea that is scientifically outdated, an
obsolete presupposition. These examples show that self-
understandings themselves need to be constantly demythologized since they tend to broaden evaluations of
human existence—such as man's autonomy—into cosmological statements.[27]

We have seen that the idea of a closed human existence is the result of an arbitrary judgment which cannot then be a necessary criterion for criticism of the gospel. The same applies even more sharply to evaluations like the enhanced significance of race or people, which are no more than social myths.

If a leading physicist today can say that science is just as compatible with religious skepticism as with the doctrine of creation,[28] it is hard to see why the outlook of the New Testament should have to agree with the self-understanding of modern man and his value judgments on the basis of human autonomy. At this point we see evaluation poised against evaluation. The gospel starts with the testimony that God resists the evaluations of autonomous man, and exactly in so doing achieves the deliverance of man.

A final example will make this clear. Presupposing man's self-understanding as a standard for criticism of the gospel, Bultmann is led to say that man "knows that he is independent and responsible for his mastery over nature."[29] In this regard one might consider what Bultmann had to say about the philosopher's hope that the character of being as a gift might be found in being itself, and then conclude with Bultmann that that seemed to be rather a counsel of despair.[30] Indeed, despair of man's independence and the results of his dominion over nature is highly in place today. On both counts, we are faced with a question of decision, and Bultmann here seems to opt for an optimistic view of man's place in the cosmos, although he rejects this in the case of his philosophical opponent.

The self-evident and responsible dominion of man over nature is a thesis, the truth of which seems to be increasingly dubious. The more technology advances, the more the uncertainty of this assertion increases for "responsible" people.

In a powerful essay on the meaning of enlightened thinking[31] Georg Picht, the Heidelberg philosopher and educational reformer, describes the course of independent and self-responsible thought from the Enlightenment to our own time. He shows how enlightened thinking, freeing itself from religion for the sake of a free moral ordering of human action, adopted a belief in the light of reason, but lost itself in the movement from Kant to Hegel and Nietzsche. Modern philosophy is more or less concerned with obscure details; responsible judgments concerning the way man rules nature are the very last thing it can give. "Enlightenment" now comes only on the "couch" of the psychiatrist, and the thrust of automatic development, research, and production has replaced moral evaluations of human action. Where Bultmann thought he saw responsibility in areas of ethics and morals, today we find irresponsibility, erosion, and at best the cry for a recovery of the concept of responsibility from some other source. Picht, for one, argues that only the Christian message, which has been rejected, can be this other source, as the concept of responsibility was originally derived from it.

This shows that it is out of place today to think that an idea of confident self-awareness, of "unity" and responsibility in man, can serve as a criterion for the gospel. For a generation now this confidence and self-awareness have been shattered. The gospel regards the assertion that human existence is closed and unitary as a permanent, not just a contemporary, error. The gospel rejects this assertion just as Bultmann must reject is as soon and as long as he describes the truth and authenticity of human existence as a gift which can come to man only from without by an "act of God." That in itself characterizes any notion of man's independence and self-sufficiency as erroneous.

To sum up, we cannot agree that value judgments that as such have no objective necessity can serve as criteria for criticism of the Christian message. This message itself has a system of value judgments which the Christian adopts by his decision, which he represents to himself, against himself, and over against others, and which claim objectivity in the sense of material correspondence to the basic facts of human existence — a claim which Bultmann readily concedes to Heidegger's existential philosophy.

At this point we have judgment against judgment, or rather, as the Christian believes and is prepared to show, the valuations of modern self-understanding against an evaluation of the objective laws of life, ideology against reality. This conflict is unavoidable. The materialist does not attempt to reconcile his views to those of idealism. According to him, idealism must and will be shattered by his thinking; the two cannot be harmonized. A communist can hardly survive if he adopts as his presupposition the self-understanding of the capitalist and his evaluation of communism. For him, the antagonism is self-evident and necessary, for in his eyes the capitalist self-understanding is harmful to man. In the same way the self-understanding of modern man, with its concept of the closed, unitary, and self-responsible nature of human existence, must be rejected because it is an illusion (Eph. 4:24) and because it is an inappropriate self-understanding, as the discussion of the autonomous responsibility of man has already shown.

Bultmann's program announces the rule of an alien ideology in the church.[32]

Demythologization and the way to atheism

A second criticism of the program of demythologization concerns its method of New Testament criticism. This method must be discussed in terms of *presuppositions, execution,* and *results.*

1. PRESUPPOSITIONS OF THE METHOD
An essential presupposition of this method of criticism is that the object to be criticized must be subsumed under the concept of myth. *Hence Greek stories of the gods and the proclamation of the New Testament are all rolled into one.* Their

obvious differences are irrelevant to the program of demythologization. This is why Bultmann speaks of the "mythology" of the New Testament.[33] Both are brought under
the law that the true point of myth is anthropological rather
than cosmological; it is to be interpreted existentially.
Demythologizing seeks to bring out the true intention of
myth: to speak about human existence.[34]

Bultmann's concept of myth corresponds to what one of
his students (whom Bultmann quotes with approval) called
hypostatizing.[35] This concept becomes, for Bultmann, a
decisive instrument of demythologizing. Some might find it
surprising that the same category can be made to comprise
both the incarnation of God in Jesus and the so utterly
different Greek myths, and that both are then treated in the
same way.[36] But the same approach is found in Bultmann's
disciple, Herbert Braun. He identifies the facticity of the
New Testament story with the facticity found elsewhere in
antiquity when, for example, it speaks of "Zeus begetting
children with women . . . or of Hekate, appearing in a forest
ravine, 300 feet high, her feet dragons, her hair serpents."[37]

Impossible, one would think. Is there no difference
between the resurrection of Jesus Christ from the dead and
the serpentine hair of a deity in Greek myth? Surely their
"facticity" is not the same. Can we simply ignore the
difference in the content of revelation? The moral and
spiritual qualities displayed by Jesus, the combination of
mercy and righteousness which Christianity sees to be the
revelation of God's nature—these can hardly be set in the
same series as the sexual activities of Zeus. Bultmann
himself is aware of the difference. In distinction from the
cultic myths of the Hellenic and Hellenistic gods he finds in
the Christ event a unique intermingling of the historical and
the mythical. But then he thinks "the contradictions" in the
New Testament, this unique intermingling, is just the
problem: it presents difficulties to understanding. He concludes that this intermingling of historical and mythical is

perhaps designed to simply express the significance of the historical figure of Jesus as a salvation figure.[38]

Thus the very distinction of the New Testament, its unique, historical and concrete particularity, is to be set aside because it conflicts with "modern self-understanding." The "mythical" material of the New Testament is not to obstruct the understanding (whose understanding?) of its *meaning,* any more than the unhistorical Greek myth prevents our apprehending its *significance.* In Bultmann's method, the organic connection between myth and history is sundered, as is history from meaning.

The content of divine revelation, however, cannot be sundered from history without perverting everything. We confess that Jesus Christ was a fully real man and not a god on a visit. We can point to the time and the place: at that time, under Pontius Pilate. We call upon a historical background which myth never has. Myths do not have a similar content or concrete reference.

If the New Testament presents actions which take place not in hidden forest ravines but in public and particular historical settings, then why the urgency to call the New Testament myth? What annoys Bultmann is that the intermingling of the mythical and the historical implies the intermingling of this world and the beyond. Finally, for Bultmann, the only common denominator for the incarnation and the dragon fact of Greek myth is the awkward, inappropriate, surprisingly impersonal and abstract formula that the other world is made into this world.[39]

It is the compulsion of the modern self-understanding that brings such dissimilar things together. Bultmann has his own concept of myth. As a result he is unable or unwilling to distinguish, as the discipline of history of religion demands, between Greek myth and New Testament proclamation. For Bultmann, myth is not a genre like saga, legend, and the like, but a decisive, philosophical classification expressing the secular presupposition that events in the world are uniform and closed to the beyond. The category of myth is the instrument with which he enforces his presupposition of an either/or of immanence and transcendence.

According to one critic, Bultmann's view of myth is not historical but philosophical or, more precisely, ontological and epistemological. It originates not from the study of comparative religion, but from existentialist philosophy and the ontological antithesis it creates between objective and non-objective thought.[40] Whenever religious statements include objective reality, argues Bultmann, we have myth. Obvious differences in religion are ignored. This critic also shows how Bultmann's stance is influenced by the intellectual situation at the beginning of the century. Both theology and philosophy then had to define a sphere in which they could exist unhampered by the scientific view of reality. They also had to overcome the relativizing of all intellectual statements by a consistently historical approach. Existentialism tried to get around historicism with its dialectic of objective and non-objective-appellative statements.[41] This is why Bultmann tries so hard to find in theology a non-objective form of expression that would not collide with the monism of the objective view of the world.

All myths then, no matter what they say, must be stories of the coming of the other-worldly into the this-worldly, or the transition of the non-objective into the objective. Hence demythologization is to be understood and pursued primarily as deobjectification.[42]

2. THE METHOD AND ITS EXECUTION: A MODEL

In *The New Testament and Myth*, Bultmann illustrates the execution of his program by applying his method to the New Testament doctrine of the Holy Spirit.[43] The Holy Spirit is a phenomenon in which the other-worldly is brought to immanent reality. This "myth" of the Holy Spirit, as Bultmann therefore calls it, is not to be *eliminated* under the pressure of the closed modern view of the world. Rather, it is to be *interpreted* in immanent terms. The point or meaning of what Scripture describes as an intervention of the transcendent into this world is that the Spirit is the "how" of existence in faith.[44] Thus, the Holy Spirit is turned into an attribute, a quality of human existence, not an object which the modern understanding of the world might dispute.[45]

Bultmann's method is characterized at the outset by an opposition between faith and psychic phenomena (which would be objective, immanent realities), only faith being the mark of the Christian life. When this principle is applied to the Holy Spirit, the Spirit is deobjectified:

> Of course Paul shares the popular view of his age that the Spirit manifests himself in miracles. . . . The Spirit is a mysterious something in man. . . . The Spirit can even be thought of as a kind of supernatural material (I Cor. 15:44f.). It is plain, however, that at root Paul understands the "Spirit" to be the factual possibility of a new life which is opened up in faith. The Spirit does not work as a natural force, but is the factual possibility of life which must be grasped in decision. "Being led by the Spirit" (Rom. 8:14) is not a natural process, but a fulfillment of the imperative not to live after the flesh. For the imperative stands in unity with the indicative. . . . Thus the concept of "Spirit" is demythologized.[46]

This statement contains three typical features of what might be called the grammar of demythologizing. To begin with, Bultmann thinks that the content of proclamation in Paul takes both a theological and an anthropological form. Bultmann first compares and then identifies the theological form with "natural force." But the introduction of the idea of a "natural force" is misleading. The question is rather one of gift, of intervention from above, of the act of God over against a human possibility that can be grasped. Bultmann's reference to a natural force is a rhetorical device that drives the reader away from Paul's idea of a special power at work in man to an exclusively anthropological statement about the possibility of new life. For as the reader will easily see, the idea of a natural force does not correspond at all to Paul's intent. It is not difficult to understand, however, how this fictional alternative is being built up. What is at first a power that *works like nature*—nature is just an analogy or comparison at first here—becomes later *a natural power.* Similarity becomes identity. Then natural power becomes a natural process—a course of things which is regular and automatic. But the Spirit is never described in these terms in the Christian tradition. The alternative set up by Bultmann is a caricature designed to lead the reader where Bultmann wants him to go.

In Paul's proclamation the work of the Holy Spirit has both theological and anthropological relevance. In Bultmann's interpretation the theological statement is dropped, or rather it is reduced to what, for Paul, was the accompanying anthropological statement. This reduction is inevitable, of course, once it is presupposed that "at root" the anthropological statement represents Paul's own meaning. This is only consistent with the ruling principle that myth really is simply a statement about human existence.

Second, corresponding to the duality of the theological and anthropological is the duality of the indicative and the imperative. The Pauline indicative that the Spirit manifests himself in miraculous acts is now reduced to an anthropological statement, to an imperative for man who has to grasp the new possibility of life. The imperative which in Paul *followed* the indicative of the gospel now has to carry both contents, including what was previously portrayed as the miraculous act of the Spirit of God.

This reduction of the indicative to the imperative, or identification of the two, is supposedly established by the vague statement that the imperative "stands in unity" with the indicative. Paul certainly teaches such a unity. But Paul relates the two in such a way that some statements are first

made in the indicative and then their contents are turned
into the respective imperative. Thus, if we *live* in the Spirit
(if we are set in the new life by God's gift), we are to *walk* in
the Spirit. In no case, however, are the indicative and the
imperative one and the same for Paul as they are for
Bultmann.

Bultmann's merging of the indicative and the imperative,
of God's work and man's, of the theological statement and
the anthropological statement, may also be seen in the fact
that the passive and the active now become interchangeable.
Being led by the Spirit is now the same thing as *not living*
after the flesh, which is something man himself can do as a
subject in the active sense.

All these are signs that the theological statements of the
New Testament have been *reduced* to anthropological statements. The degree to which Bultmann sees the theological
and anthropological statements as *alternatives* may be seen
from the recurring "not . . . but" pattern of his argument. In
Paul the theological and anthropological statements are set
side by side, in this order, as the nature of God's work in the
world demands. But because Bultmann presupposed that
their content is identical, he reduces the theological statements to anthropological statements, thus eliminating the
theological category.

A final decisive characteristic of the grammar of demythologizing is the changing of the finite verb into a mere
"is." Whereas Paul says that the Spirit works, Bultmann
simply says that the Spirit "is" (the possibility of life). *This is
the central manipulation. For only by cutting out the finite verb
can theological statements be reduced to anthropological statements.* A finite verb establishes the precedence of the subject. "Is" merely expresses the equality of subject and
predicate: the Spirit "is" the factual possibility of life; being
led by the Spirit "is" the fulfillment of the imperative—by
man. A theological statement is now an anthropological
statement, myth is a statement about existence, and a

statement about the other world is a statement about this world.

This equation is the presupposition for the next step. The two sides of an equation are of course interchangeable. What was first the predicate can become the subject, and what was first the subject can become the predicate. By this interchange man's work can replace what was originally God's work. This shift is palpable in Bultmann.[47] For in Paul's saying about being led by the Spirit, God is the subject, while man is the subject of not living any longer according to the flesh. *But in Bultmann the original predicate threatens to swallow up the subject, and in the end the statement about God's work is completely lost and only one about man's work remains. The result is, in effect, atheism.*

If the finite verb had been kept we should read that the Holy Spirit *creates* the "factual possibility of life." This would keep the proper emphasis, preserve the two elements, and uphold the New Testament order. The equation made by the "is," however, removes the priority of the divine work and subject. A mere "is"—and this is what Bultmann aims at—finally amounts to no more than "means."

The shift establishing the precedence of the human subject may also be seen when Bultmann speaks of the faith which works by love, saying that this attitude means to be a new creature.[48] The secret identification of man's being (by God's creation) and his acting has already been subjected to such an exchange that man's action in this world becomes the subject. It then simply receives a new name ("means") designed to preserve the theological element. The priority of the human subject and the reduction of the theological statement to an anthropological statement are plain to see.

The "mythological" (or theological!) assertion is then simply another name and does not refer to any new content—as is shown by the identity of transcendence and immanence posited by the copula, "is." It is merely an extra name for the same anthropological situation.[49] *In effect, demythologizing means to anthropologize theology.*

3. THE METHOD OF DEMYTHOLOGIZATION: A PARALLEL TO FEUERBACH'S ATHEISTIC CRITICISM OF RELIGION

Those familiar with the critical method of Ludwig Feuerbach, the forefather of all modern criticism of religion, will have observed its striking similarity to the method of Bultmann's demythologization program.

There is, first, a parallel between Bultmann's concept of myth (myth as the expression of man's understanding of existence in cosmological categories) and the methodological presupposition of Feuerbach's criticism of religion. Religion, for Feuerbach, is man's consciousness of his own nature. "For me the infinite is simply the essence of the finite." Feuerbach's underlying principle is already expressed in his early *Thoughts on Death and Immortality:* "The I makes itself an object."

Immanence and transcendence and "the finite and the infinite" are the effective sets of terms in Feuerbach, and Hans Jonas's idea that myth is the expression of "hypostatized" human experiences is already present in Feuerbach as a central concept of his criticism of religion: it hails from Kant's critique of the proofs for the existence for God.

There is also a parallel between Bultmann and Feuerbach in the preparation of the material. Both sever the connection between the mythical and the historical and bring all religious statements under the master concept of myth. This preparation is necessary for the success of the method. Bultmann and Feuerbach first banish the historical element from Christianity: the distinction between timeless myths and history which can be localized to specific persons and times must be expunged. Having banished the historical element, they can then criticize or interpret the "meaning."

In both thinkers, this preparation leads to the reduction of finite verbs (which denote events or history) to mere "is" sayings. "Is" sayings express states or eternal truths, and in them any *transition* from the other world to this world, or vice versa, is eliminated. Bultmann's criticism of Paul's doctrine of the Holy Spirit has a striking similarity to Feuerbach's reduction of the biblical notion of man as the image of God. The biblical verb sentence "God made man in his own image" is first exchanged for an "is" saying: "Man is the image of God." If it is then forgotten that this latter phrase is only the secondary and reduced form of a statement with a finite verb, likeness or analogy can become identity, and the two sides of the equation are interchanged: "God is the image of man." In an "is" statement the subject and predicate can be reversed; in a theological "is" statement God and man, theology and anthropology, can be reversed. Feuerbach (and Marx) also speaks of the need to exchange subject and predicate in the statements of theology and (idealistic) philosophy. Finally, since equation means identity, and therefore is a tautology, one side can be reduced to the other. The predicate swallows up its original subject.[50]

This manipulation occurs in Bultmann as well as in Feuerbach. *But whereas Feuerbach plainly says that he is replacing theology by anthropology and that atheism is the result, Bultmann still passionately defends his theology against any such characterization.*

4. DEMYTHOLOGIZING MEANS ALLEGORIZING

Feuerbach as well as Bultmann thinks of a negative as well as a positive aspect of his criticism. Feuerbach cannot be accused of being a merely destructive critic, of merely having eliminated transcendence and theology. As Bultmann goes beyond the demythologizing of myths to an existential interpretation, so Feuerbach wants to make the conclusions of his criticism the premises of a new philosophy of humanism. Both Feuerbach and Bultmann attempt reinterpretation: each is convinced that he can find the "true" meaning or the deeper purpose of the traditional statements.

Bultmann's definition of myth already implies a program

of reinterpretation. The material has to be given another meaning: i.e. it has to be allegorized. This is shown by the expressions "strictly" and "at root," and by the dominant position given to the word "meaning" and later to the science of hermeneutics. It is true that at the beginning of his 1941 essay Bultmann rejects any resolution of the conflict between the gospel and the modern self-understanding along the lines of an allegorizing of the biblical message which would seek its true meaning in the life of the soul or in man's inwardness.[51] Nor is the act of God to be found in psychic phenomena. We have seen that Bultmann himself gives to the act of God a location which has nothing to do with time and space (even the time and space of the soul) in the cosmological sense. His anthropologizing is a complete deobjectification. Thus it is an even more far-reaching abstraction than any earlier one. Nonetheless, an allegory is the result. With his program of demythologizing, Bultmann has inaugurated a new era of allegorizing in which the expositor brings with him his own "guiding concepts," putting the gospel into these new terms. This opens the door to arbitrary exposition and the dominion of man over the message—the trademark of all allegorizing.

5. BULTMANN'S TALK ABOUT GOD'S ACT
AND HIS ATTEMPT TO AVOID ATHEISM
In two ways, however, Bultmann distinguishes himself from Feuerbach. First, he claims that he very differently presents theology as anthropology: that is, he views theological statements as statements about, or in, existence.[52] He also argues that his interpretation can be called anthropological only if anthropology is understood as an existential analysis of human life, not an objectifying anthropology which regards human existence only as a phenomenon in the world.[53] In this regard he parts company with Feuerbach. If Feuerbach's thinking is rightly anthropological and this-worldly, it is still wrongly objective. In contrast, Bultmann champions a non-objective anthropology. Indeed, Feuerbach thought that he had to understand man, in his varied

interrelation with nature, corporeality, and society, first and foremost as a "phenomenon of the world." Whether Bultmann, with his own addition of anthropologizing and deobjectification, has really chosen the better part will be discussed in the next chapter, "The Surrender of Reality: Repercussions of Bultmann's Approach." So far we have only seen a variation within the commitment to anthropology.

Second, Bultmann tries to show how far he is from atheism by referring to the "act of God" as a typical feature in the Christian message, thus distinguishing the Christian message from all philosophy. The definition of both the old man and the new, says Bultmann, permitted and demanded the reduction of theology to anthropology, but *the change* from the old life of man to his new life could be understood only in terms of an act of God. It was a salvation event which separates the two, and which could be reduced to the possibilities or realities available to man. If this were not so, the new life could be achieved quite apart from God and his saving act. The New Testament would then simply bring to light and expression a natural understanding of the being of man which the garb of myth had concealed. Theology would then be outshone by philosophy.

Does Bultmann succeed in demonstrating the need for this special factor, the act of God? His exposition of the transition from the pre-Christian to the Christian self-understanding begins with the observation that philosophy maintains man's own ability to make this qualitative leap into the new life ("You can if you must"), whereas Christian faith says that the new life, or authenticity of existence, comes to man only as a gift.[54] The crucial point, for Bultmann, lies precisely here. Being can be understood as a gift only when the love of God encounters man as an embracing and sustaining power.[55] Faith is man's freedom from self and his openness to the future. Faith is man's authenticity; and faith is possible only as faith in the love of God.

Why is this? Bultmann gives as his reason the fact that only he who is already loved can love. Only he who has received trust can give trust. Only he who has experienced self-giving can give himself.[56] In sum, the decisive thing that differentiates Christian faith from natural self-understanding is the "act of God" which first makes man's authentic life possible.[57]

We obviously have a leap in logic here. It is hard to see why a giver should have to be inferred from the character of being as a gift, and on top, that it should be God. It is hard to see why the embracing and sustaining power which is sought should have to be the love of—God. It is hard to see why the character of *being* as a gift should necessarily imply a preceding *act,* and an act of God. Is this not exactly an example of a "basic experience and motif" in real life, which produces a dogmatic hypostatizing just as described by Jonas? Indeed, we have in fact a new mythologizing which criticism will unmask as a translation of this world into the form of the world beyond. This is arbitrary, because a very different, *immanent* answer could well be given. D. von Oppen, a German sociologist, provides us with an astonishing parallel to these deliberations, but he refers to a more plausible answer—the love that is already present in this world. One's unconditional acceptance and affirmation by another person, as seen in a family or in a mother's love which does not falter, even when one fails, can be the this-worldly source of sustainment and achievement.[58]

Bultmann's student, Herbert Braun, gets closer to the truth. His famous formulation refers simply to a "source of upholding" rather than to God. In contrast, at this decision point, Bultmann again employs something that he has previously defined as myth, speaking of love as the love of God, even defining this love in terms of an act of God, and finally linking this act of God to the historical person of Jesus of Nazareth. These statements involve successive steps of re-concretizing—reobjectification. True, they are gospel statements. But they no longer stand in any real relation to the announced purpose of Bultmann's program.

Bultmann is conscious of this rift. He puts the question to himself: "Are there still any surviving traces of mythology?"[59] His answer is that there are for those who consider any talk about God to be mythological. But mythology in his presentation was not the same as traditional mythology. For the relation of the act of God to the historical particularity of Jesus of Nazareth was sufficiently balanced by the description of the cross and resurrection as an "eschatological event" in the "ongoing present." Here Bultmann wants to accommodate Dilthey's principle that dogmas are untenable when understood as restricted to the facts of Christian history, whereas when understood in their universal sense they denote the supremely living content of all history.[60] For Dilthey is offended by the rigid, exclusive reference to the person of Jesus that expressly rules out all other references. Bultmann thus recognizes that the event-character of the gospel is a scandal for philosophical thought. He therefore seeks a dimension for the act of God in which this act is not particular or unique in its facticity but an ongoing present, an "eschatological event," a generality which does not refer everything to a single, scandalizing, historical place and point in time.

An "act" but no facticity—this contradiction defines in brief the dilemma that ends the attempt to differentiate the program of demythologization from atheism. If the desired demythologization succeeds, theology is redundant. If it does not, the conflict with the modern self-understanding persists.

6. The development of the program in the direction of atheism

Bultmann's presentation could not stand still—it had either to advance or to retreat. The Czech theologian J. B. Soucek at once raised the objection: "When I think of my secularized acquaintances, for them any reference to the cross as an eschatological event which applies to every age and is present in every age is pure and simple mythology. It is so, at least, when it is meant seriously and is not meant as a mere symbol for the structure of existence." Gustav Wingren had a similar objection to Bultmann's view: "The forgiveness of sins, considered as an act of God, is just as unacceptable as the resurrection considered as an act of God."[61]

Fritz Buri of Basel was the one who above all detected the intrinsic contradiction in Bultmann and demanded the advance to understanding the gospel as a *mere* symbol of the structure of existence.[62] Buri contests Bultmann's starting-point: in the New Testament the self-understanding is based on mythical events which are presupposed to be reality. The starting-point is not that the events are an "expression of the self-understanding." Buri points out that Bultmann reversed the original relation between event and meaning, giving primacy to meaning. He is all the more astonished then that Bultmann should still think it necessary to tie the timeless possibility of a new self-understanding to a specific salvation event.[63] After taking a step forward, Bultmann now takes a step back. The logical result of his de-mythologizing ought to be a dekerygmatizing of theology, which completely separates the preaching of the new self-understanding from the delusion of exclusiveness which insists on the uniqueness of a divine act of salvation in Jesus Christ. As Buri puts it, the salvation event is not limited either to the New Testament, the Bible, or the Christian community. He reiterates what D. F. Strauss had already formulated when he said that "the idea" does not like to lavish its fullness in one example. Salvation does not hang on one point in history.[64] Bultmann is inconsistent when he speaks of a timeless act of God and in some way relates this again to the events around Jesus of Nazareth.

What is offensive in the particularity of the salvation event is that it conflicts with the idea of eternal recurrence in the myths of antiquity. It also forms the climax of the mythical thinking of the New Testament. This historical particularity causes far more offense than anything in other myths. It is not the event-character that constitutes the offense in the gospel. "Events" (*Geschehen*) can still be interpreted in terms of the constant present—an ongoing process rather than history. From this no conflict need arise with the immanent understanding of the cosmos as we find it in secularism. The real offense in the New Testament is not only the proclamation of a resurrection, but already that a specific person should be preached. The "then" of God's act, its particularity, is the point of conflict. If God's "act" simply denotes ontological relations, structures of existence, or the constant changes that are conceivable in them, there is no need for alarm. But if the uniqueness, particularity, and quasi-contingency of an event is proclaimed which implies election of God and the bondage of man, the call to battle is sounded. In the eyes of secular man, this particularity, and the mythical God who stands behind it, must be rejected. It needs to be translated into the so-called modern self-understanding of man.[65]

Herbert Braun, the most radical representative of Bultmann's school, seems to be willing to go all the way. (His "theology" interests us here only in so far as it discloses and avoids the contradictions in Bultmann, and not for the moment in its bearing on theism or atheism.) Braun deliberately adopts the standpoint of modern man and wants to share his philosophical presuppositions, including the presupposition that the cosmos is a closed network of causality. Hence, he cannot accept any idea of a God out there or a God who intervenes, whether in past revelation or in the future. For the modern age, he says, the "apocalyptic picture of the world" has gone.[66]

Braun rightly sees what is the basic question in modern theological discussion: the concept of reality. In a lecture on "The Salvation Facts of the New Testament," given as part of a series on "Object and Objectivity in Science" at the

University of Mainz in 1959-1960, he gives greater precision to the problem Bultmann was working on. He says that
we cannot divide reality into two parts, as many theologians still do, in order to preserve the objectivity of
salvation events. We should not isolate certain events and
make of them a reality different from the everyday one in
which we deal with causal sequences. The great field of
reality has to be investigated as a whole. It can be investigated in this way because it is subject to laws which are
either known already or will be known in the future. A
miracle in the ancient sense—the intervention of a divine
being in the normal course of events—is ruled out for
modern thinking. But some theologians still carve out a
little sphere for another reality where the normal rules do
not apply. Here, two times two can be five. These theologians have a double concept of reality. But this division
ruins the idea of honest knowledge, for it does not take
secular reality seriously. The unity of reality cannot be
surrendered.[67] For this reason, Braun intends to stay resolutely within the this-worldly sphere and regard this sphere
as closed whether in relation to natural law or history.[68]

Though he shares a common presupposition with
Bultmann, Braun is more consistent and precise in his
definition of what Bultmann called the embracing and
sustaining power. Illogically, Bultmann went on to speak of
"God" in this connection; respecting the presuppositions of
secularism, Braun more accurately comes up with the
formula "the whence of my being upheld." The content of
this "whence" is necessarily imprecise. To call it God is an
arbitrary positing or traditional naming, a renewed transcending that is not demanded by, and does not impart, any
new material element. Also, along the lines of Bultmann's
demythologization of the New Testament view of the Holy
Spirit, but pressing further, Braun no longer speaks of God
himself in terms of action (Bultmann's "act of God") or in
terms of a center of action—an acting subject, a person.

God can be referred to only in terms of being.[69] He is not the self-existent one. Rather, as a "how" of being or an attribute of human existence, God must be "a kind of fellow-humanity."[70] God does not *do* anything. God or Jesus "is" or "happens." God "expresses"[71] or "stands for"[72] phenomena of human life which can be described in terms of this world. Thus Braun reaches the same result as does Bultmann's demythologizing of the Holy Spirit: A person of the Godhead becomes a "how" of human existence.

"God," then, is only a manner of speaking. The tautological character of the term—and all tautologies are strictly superfluous—is palpable in the grammatical impossibility of a statement from the pen of so fine a writer as Braun: "God is the whence . . . in terms of fellow-man."[73] Braun himself confirms our findings when he says that all the traditional themes of theology—including the salvation event in relation to which Bultmann still maintained that a reference to an "act of God" could not be avoided—can in fact be handled without any use of the term "God."[74]

Is the Christian message differentiated from philosophy by specific content—a content that Bultmann still found in the transition from the old man to the new? Braun answers No. The authenticity of man does not come as a new creation through an act of God. This may be inferred when Braun says that "man as man"—obviously in his natural possibility and actuality—"implies God."[75] In clearcut terms and with no "remnant of mythology," he states that God is a concept of anthropology, and without the hedging of Bultmann he states forthrightly that theology must be anthropology.

Braun's position supports our observation that consistent demythologizing must finish up close to the atheism of Feuer-bach. For Feuerbach's criticism of religion it was essential that there should be an inversion of God and man, or theology and anthropology. We find the same in Braun in a statement which is significant for method: "Anthropology is the constant; christology is the variable."[76] Theology is a variable expression for basic anthropological facts.

Finally, Braun has done away with the contradictions and caprice inherent in Bultmann's theological position by consistently seeking and finding the power that embraces and sustains man within the "closed nexus of the world." "Security and duty do not come to me from the cosmos but from the other, from my fellow-man; even the word of proclamation and the act of love come to me . . . from my fellow-man. God is the whence of my security and commitment in terms of my fellow-man."[77]

What we have here is a secular doctrine of grace, a doctrine of salvation without christology or theology. In the nineteenth century another "cultural theology" attempted to demonstrate the abiding worth of the Bible to a critical age by distilling eternal truths out of the biblical stories and concepts. At this point, Braun's theology is simply the old theological liberalism, except that now existential and quasi-immanent religious experiences are abstracted from the Bible rather than general truths. It is a return of Schleiermacher. Perhaps one might also say that a bit of the pietist tradition is worked in from August Tholuck and Wilhelm Herrmann. Christian faith is not reduced to a moral imperative, but in good Herrmann style, the question is raised of the *possibility* of morality or the power to love. Bultmann answers this question by referring to an "act of God" on man. Braun answers it by talk of being upheld by fellow-man: "God is the kind of fellow-humanity which is empowered for love by encounter."[78]

But is this not pure humanism? Of course it is, says Braun. The only thing that needs to be added is the gift-aspect. Say "liberating love" instead of humanism and you are already at the heart of the New Testament. And if we remember that all fellow-humanity shares in this receiving and giving and hence in what the New Testament describes, we may conclude that there is no need to be alarmed at the cry that theology is now dissolved in humanism.[79]

Such a view, which might be described as a skillful anthropologizing and secularizing of the biblical doctrine of law and gospel, might well be seen as a correction of existing secular humanist tradition, for which one ought to be grateful. But from a Christian point of view, the question remains: How does this preaching differ from atheistic humanism?

Braun thinks the question is a legitimate one and he tries to answer it. He thinks his own position is *beyond* both theism and atheism—positions which, given his message, are stale and unprofitable.[80] He thus argues that they have no significance for him and bear no relation to what he is trying to say.

Braun tries to avoid atheism by asking whether there are any atheists anyway—if God is this kind of fellow-humanity in encounter, of which all men have some experience.[81] However, if theism and atheism, or God and no God, are irrelevant from this standpoint, the question arises with what right Braun, too, continues to call what he has in mind "God." Especially so as he says elsewhere, in a sentence which corresponds point by point to the religious criticism of Feuerbach and Marx, that from the standpoint of theism, God represents an empty shell into which each of its proponents packs his own contents.[82] If Braun's criticism of theism is turned against himself when he calls the fulfillment of fellow-humanity "God," Braun in fact is proving that in his "theology," too, it is superfluous to talk about God. For if the term "God" is an empty shell, why should we still use it?

This is precisely the objection Hellmut Gollwitzer brings against Braun.[83] He brings Braun face to face with a Marxist atheist who is not encumbered by the Christian tradition. This Marxist could accept without modification all that he is told by Braun about true fellow-humanity. But what is the reason, he would ask, for retaining the outdated and hopelessly mythological word "God"? The theologian who tries to foist it on him is typically a man who stands between the past and the present, making demands which admittedly have no basis. With good reason theologians who think like Braun can be asked why they will not accept the straightforward atheistic vocabulary of Marxism as far more honest and up-to-date. For obviously the only point of difference now is one of vocabulary. The introduction of the word "God" does not add to our knowledge. If "God" is just a particular form of fellow-humanity, Braun is at one with Feuerbach and therefore with the atheists. The only change he can ask of them is that they use another term for something they are already agreed upon. Braun's exposition of the New Testament message might persuade a Marxist that the Bible has a positive humanist core. But in no way will this lead him to any kind of belief in God. It will simply confirm his view that such a view is unnecessary.[84] In sum, compared to the biblical knowledge of God, this agnosticism is atheism.[85]

Those who have even a slight acquaintance with the theory of Marxist atheism must agree that Gollwitzer's comparison of it to Braun is valid. In both cases the reality of God, his entry into the world, the creation, and the divine sonship of Jesus are contested. In both cases we have "transcendence" without any heavenly transcendence (Bloch). Marxism is soberly content with human truths. Braun, in contrast, demands the use of another name, "God," as the renewed hypostatizing of a human reality. He suffers from what Feuerbach called the Christian "disease of seeing": He wants to see more than is actually there. He tries to avoid the criticism of Marxism, which exposes his purely semantic distinction as a mere superstructure and reduces it to its real basis. Marxism here raises the "ideological suspicion." It will not concede any separate existence to theological atheism. This would be a luxury. It would be the philosophical "Indian Reservation" which Braun says he does not want. A disguised atheism of this kind—Christianity as "humanism plus mystery"—presents the Christian faith on a silver platter for final destruction by the Marxist criticism of religion.[86]

2

THE SURRENDER OF REALITY:

Repercussions of Bultmann's Approach

THE QUESTION AND CONCEPTS: A PARTICULAR PHILOSOPHY AS MANDATORY PREAMBLE

BULTMANN'S PROGRAM FOR REINTERPRETING the Christian message presupposes the clash of the traditional forms of the Christian message with the modern world view and self-understanding. The modern thought forms into which the kerygma is to be poured so as to be understandable to modern men are to be provided by Heidegger's existentialist philosophy. According to Bultmann, existentialism represents *the* authentic version of man's modern self-understanding, and thus provides the specific set of questions and concepts by which every interpretation of Scripture today must be guided.[1] Bultmann assumes that in the church, at least, the question of *existence,* toward which we are driven by our own lives, is the most suitable approach to studying the Bible.[2] Thus, existentialism attains the rank of being *the* appropriate system of philosophy.

By establishing the question in this way the field of

exposition clearly becomes restricted and controlled. But, retorts Bultmann, methodological interpretation is needed if we are to understand a text. Certain rules must apply. Exegetical work must depend on philosophical work; this is a necessary technical presupposition for Bultmann.[3] However, he claims that the concepts guiding his exposition derive from a philosophy which is the *right* one (he says) because it expresses the theory that exactly corresponds to human existence as such. Bultmann seems to assume that existentialism is the only possible understanding of existence; that it simply is the voice of human existence itself. Therefore he can make the "guiding concepts" of his exposition.

But in face of Bultmann's usually complicated deliberations it is unlikely and indeed impossible that there should be a philosophy which is quite simply the right one because it expresses human existence in suitable concepts with full objectivity and fidelity. Is there in fact only one understanding of existence that corresponds to its subject? Only one appropriate exposition of existence? If so, then existence would speak to us unequivocally. But it doesn't. At so decisive a point we must not reduce the whole supply of presuppositions to one set of suitable concepts by adopting a single specific philosophical view. The question of existence muzzles the other answers that the gospel may have to give. In addition, the gospel may even have its own ideas of what existence is. What is to happen if, when philosophy has been allowed to delimit the field of human existence, "existence" is saying or asking something the gospel calls a lie, a false question, or human revolt? An uncritical pre-insertion of philosophy will initiate a thrust toward the distortion, abbreviation, or allegorization of the gospel.

The philosophical concept of human existence is one such pre-insertion. It comes under the category of self-understanding, originates in human decisions, and consists of human valuations. Over against it, the gospel tells us that the evaluations and questions that genuinely correspond to reality cannot be reached apart from revelation.

For these reasons Karl Barth continually emphasized that theology must not be bound methodologically to philosophy but rather, as much as possible, derive its own theological concepts from the Bible. Otherwise a presupposed philosophical analysis of existence will finally play, as it does here, the role of a powerful—this time atheistic—natural theology and impose a straitjacket on the Christian tradition.

THE CONCEPT OF "SELF-UNDERSTANDING" AND ITS IMPLICATIONS FOR THE VIEW OF REALITY

The deobjectification—the unclothing of the gospel from its traditional forms—accomplished by Bultmann's concept of myth has been completed positively by reclothing the gospel in terms of the modern concept of "self-understanding."[4] This concept alone has far-reaching implications for a view of reality. It decides whether or not God's work is located in the world.[5] The idea of self-understanding fits well, of course, with a program of deobjectifying the biblical message. For (a) it reduces all objects to the self, as a magnitude which no longer represents an object; and (b) it reduces all activities to that of understanding, an activity that no longer affects any object.

Talking about a "new self-understanding" as a category of exposition is not in itself a bad thing. One may indeed welcome Bultmann's focusing of the New Testament message on the themes of man's renewal, the old man, the new man, and the change in quality between the two. This anthropologico-soteriological concentration brings us face to face with the central proclamation of the New Testament, and one of the central problems of our own age. In Bultmann's program, however, this renewal has no concrete actuality in space and time. Accepting the Christian message undoubtedly brings about an alteration in man's self-understanding. One may not say, however, that it does this alone and nothing else.

Bultmann seems to want to say just that, for it accords with his thesis that myth is to be expounded *only* in terms of man's self-understanding. But even in the pagan world myths are not just efforts to explain human experiences and situations. They also express cosmology: that is, they also say something about man's understanding of the world. Perhaps Bultmann's approach is already too narrow for him to see this.

Hence Barth rightly says in opposition to Bultmann that the main statements in the Christian confession do not relate merely to human existence . . . but, by their very nature, speak about God's work; hence they are full of nature and the cosmos.[6] The objects of the Christian understanding embrace more than the self.[7] They embrace the whole man and indeed the whole world. Similarly, the activities implied by Christian understanding may be more than merely intellectual.

But Bultmann's arbitrary view of myth and his narrow interpretation of the guiding concept of self-understanding both are intended to shield proclamation from the criticism of the objective world. The concept of self-understanding must forestall and disarm the objection that the gospel encroaches upon the accepted scientific view of the universe as closed. The point is that the gospel does not meddle in the things of this world. Even the historical events that are the content of the New Testament are reduced to the concepts of self-understanding. As Bultmann emphasizes, its non-demonstrability protects Christian proclamation against the charge of being mythology.[8]

The fatal reductionism is apparent here. Ostensibly seeking to save the gospel message Bultmann withdraws it from the storm of philosophical battle, but at the price of surrendering its relation to the everyday world. The gospel speaks to the believer only on the plane of self-understanding. The self is all that remains to him. Understanding of the *world* must be sought through philosophies.

Because Bultmann's concept of self-understanding thus reduces, indeed dissolves into thin air, the field of reality in which God works, it must be rejected.[9]

DEOBJECTIFICATION: LOSS OF (A) CORPOREALITY AND (B) SOCIALITY

To interpret the gospel exclusively in terms of self-understanding, as a program of deobjectification, entails a grave loss of concreteness. The events described in the Christian message are contracted to a geometrical point with no extensions and dimensions. This loss of concreteness is evident in the presentation of the gospel both as past event and as present reality: i.e. in the renewal of the believer.

The view of Jesus Christ

For Bultmann, Jesus may be understood as savior from the mere *fact* of his coming.[10] The details of his life and death are superfluous. The facts of his coming dwindle down to a single historical point with no relation to space and time, and, consequently, without corporeality or sociality. It is reduced to a pure act, to the pinpoint of a mere "that." Who he was and how he acted we need not ask. There need be no interest in the historical Jesus as revealed in the synoptic records. What is recorded there is a matter of indifference. Above all, there must be nothing objective.

But the New Testament witnesses speak differently; they all agree that the tomb of Jesus was empty on Easter morning. He was not there. If he had actually risen from the dead, as the angel said and the disciples began to believe with fear and trembling, then incontestibly the resurrection had an objective character. It was a bodily resurrection.

But Bultmann's separation of the gospel from objective reality cannot accept this. *The world of objectivity has been surrendered in principle. This is why Gustav Wingren can say that to take away the corporeality of the resurrection is possible only if corporeality has already been abandoned at all other points too.*[11]

By referring to an "act of God," Bultmann tries to avoid the charge that he is whittling away the distinction between Christian faith and general philosophical knowledge. But the mere assertion of an event about which nothing more can be said is an empty assertion.

The view of the Christian

The same abstraction controls Bultmann's sketch of the actualization of salvation in the individual Christian. What happened *then* determines with its content what is to happen *now*. If the past salvation events had no tangible content, neither does present salvation have palpable content for the believer. This too is reduced to the mere "that" of "naked faith." For those who regard the resurrection as only the interpretation of the significance of the earthly life of Jesus, rising again with Christ likewise logically implies no real change in life but only a change in the way of looking at life, a new way of interpreting the fact that in reality everything remains unchanged. The resurrection of Christ and the renewal of the Christian correspond to one another. As the body of Jesus remained in the tomb, so the ethical and existential quality of human life must stay the same.

The Bible, however, speaks of a real change. It speaks of a new being and a new creation, not just of a new self-understanding. In the New Testament, conversion and the ensuing walk of faith concern practice, not just thought. As the stories of Zacchaeus and the rich young ruler show, the renewal of man touches his life materially. In contrast, the guiding concepts of self-understanding reduce the demand for repentance to the mere question whether a man will *understand* himself as crucified and risen with Christ.[12] *The only change is in the understanding.* Marxism can rightly say that this reduced religion is opium. It is indeed a winding of flowers around existential chains. A theology without reality is an obvious target for Marxism's criticism of religion.

There is a self-evident difference between Jesus' demand that his disciples *crucify* themselves and Bultmann's "question" whether we will *understand* ourselves as crucified. Jesus does not say that he who would follow him must "understand" himself as crucified. To be sure, Christian conversion does entail a change in self-understanding — thus Bultmann can quote Paul's "reckon ye yourselves" in the baptismal admonition of Romans 6 to support his own removal of the object of theology from the battle of objectivity. But more than the subjective judgment of believers is at issue in Romans 6. From the new being there also follows the readiness of the "members" for good works, denoting both man's corporeality and also his practice, which are expressions and objectifications of the new self-understanding.

Ironically, a passage Bultmann uses as a basis for saying that the event of crucifixion is a constant present shows us specifically how important corporeality is: "Always bearing about *in the body* the dying of the Lord Jesus" (2 Cor. 4:10). Corporeality is the locus of the salvation events both with Christ and his followers. The New Testament leaves us in no doubt about this (cf. Matt. 5:29 and 1 Cor. 6:20: "Glorify God in your body," or John 2:21 and 1 Cor. 3:16, which speak of the temple of the body). Verses such as 1 Cor. 6:13 — "The body is not meant for immortality, but for the Lord, and the Lord for the body," so that "your bodies are members of Christ" (v. 15)[13] — show that man's corporeality and not just his self-understanding is the field of God's action and hence the realm to which Christian dogmatics and Christian ethics refer. God's work in the world takes place in a new self-understanding, too, but it takes place first in the death and resurrection of Jesus of Nazareth once and for all, in a specific historical place. Thereafter, it is effectual not just in altering man's view of himself, but, as the Apostles expressly say, "in the mighty acts of God" (Acts 2:11). *The bodily reality of man and the bodily reality of world history are the theaters of God's glory.* They are not matters of indifference. God reigns over both.[14]

The view of man

The phrase "to *understand* oneself as crucified with Christ" typifies the program of demythologization.

To use the terms of Descartes, which seem to exercise a secret control here, faith and life are matters of thought, *res cogitans* rather than *res extensa.* They are not objective and do not relate to anything objective. Bultmann adopts from existentialist philosophy more than just the attempt to avoid the attacks of an objective view of the world: At the same time he is adopting from this philosophy a revival of Descartes' division of reality.

An observation of the nature of man can remind us that the division of reality into two worlds finds visible contradiction in man himself. For man belongs to both worlds. To divide his being is to rob him of life.[15]

Hellmuth Plessner, who, with Max Scheler, has done a great deal to overcome the Cartesian cleavage of reality, rejects the idea that man can investigate his own being in isolation from all that is outside man. Instead, he argues, man finds himself as one element in a sea of being, and, despite the non-uniform character of his existence, he is part of a series with all the other things of this world.[16]

Plessner describes the being of man as "excentric

positionality"—a term not unlike Barth's theological designation of man as the soul of his body. Bultmann can also speak to the same effect in his *Theology of the New Testament*. Here he describes the relation between soul and body in the New Testament as follows. The *soma* (body) is not something external attached to the true "I" of man. It belongs essentially to this I. Hence one can say, not that man *has* a *soma*, but that he *is* soma. For fairly frequently *soma* can simply be translated "I." On the other hand, man can make himself the object of an action. He can stand at a distance from himself. Thus the inner and outer aspects of the sensory reality of the I are, to begin with, undifferentiated.[17] The same applies in Old Testament theology.

Since Bultmann's exegesis is so sound, how is it that in his programmatic essays he can speak of the indifference of the New Testament to everything external? How is it that he can also insist on the correspondence between existentialist philosophy and the New Testament in their views of man's position and mode of being in the world?

The program of deobjectification—presupposing as it does the opposition of spirit and matter as essential and unessential existence—founders above all on the reality of man himself. The impossibility of dividing spirit and matter in man as essential vs. negligible existence is acknowledged today by the trend in medicine which accepts in practice the interaction of soul and body. A doctrine of reality which does not do justice to the reality of spirit and matter in man must be dropped. Certainly the proclamation of the gospel must not be tied to such a doctrine.

Deobjectification: loss of the fellow-man (sociality)

In his profound study of the program of demythologization Heinrich Ott attacks its individualism.[18] Already Helmut Thielicke had criticized Bultmann's "guiding concept" of the "self-understanding": it was to be rejected as a solipsism, as a restriction to the sphere of the I as severed from the Thou, and hence as the cause of a breakdown in fellowship. Thielicke also drew attention to the originally social character of sin and showed that for Bultmann sin is a phenomenon of the ego, of its interior existence.[19] Wingren makes the same criticism when he says that, with Bultmann, guilt is detached from the neighbor and takes on an egocentric tinge: "I have not actualized my existence." The neighbor and his demands have to yield at this decisive point.[20]

The same criticism may be made positively in respect to the lacunae in Bultmann's doctrine of man. The concept of self-understanding teaches us to relate the other man and the whole cosmos to the I, the solitary ego. Subsequent deliberations do not change the emphasis. Where the concept of self-understanding tends to individualize man, the preaching of Jesus sets human existence in interpersonal relations: you and your brother. How far Bultmann's subjectivism is essential may be seen in his own defense against the attacks of Thielicke and others. He claims that when a new self-understanding is given "it is not just a matter of consciousness. My whole situation changes . . . the whole world appears in a new light, it becomes in fact an entirely different world."[21] This in fact reiterates the profound subjectivism of the I, in Bultmann's claim that through a change in self-understanding an actual change has been made in the world itself—when in truth I am only seeing it differently.

If it can be said only that man comes to a new understanding of himself and his situation, this means that the people around him merely are part of his situation and have significance only as such. In his attempt at a model of demythologization Bultmann spoke of the new man "being open to his fellow-man."[22] This is consistent—consistently subjective and consistently meager.

The view of reality in Bultmann

The distinctive features in Bultmann's program, which I have been ascribing to his assumed need for deobjectification, have been attributed by Heinrich Ott to Bultmann's basic twofold view of reality. Bultmann holds a twofold ontology, a double conception of reality that seems to go hand-in-hand with a certain type of existential philosophy.[23] Out of two modes of knowledge, Bultmann makes two different realities: "The complex of events in time and space which are accessible to objective contemplation, not the history in which I really stand." According to Ott, events in time and space, even those concerning man's own corporeality, are ultimately for Bultmann outside the "history in which man really stands." By reason of this double principle Bultmann can no longer unite *the reality of meaning* (the "history" in which I really stand) and *the reality of corporeality.* Belonging to time and space, corporeality must be exiled to the plane of historical objectivity. It is this presupposition that calls for the contesting of the bodily resurrection of Jesus.[24] For Bultmann, the content of myth belongs only to the sphere of non-objective statements. When myth offers a this-worldly account of the other-worldly, it makes a transition from the one sphere of reality to the other. It thus breaches the closed picture of objective reality and asserts something that has not taken place and cannot take place in the objective world of time and space.[25]

The point at issue is the possibility or impossibility of certain judgments of reality. Bultmann assumes that this world and the other world, as two ontologically different spheres of reality, must be kept apart. If this is true, it must be highly disturbing to him that in the history of thought we find statements that crassly intermingle the two and still claim to represent reality. This claim must in principle be denied to them so far as objective reality is concerned.[26] The resurrection of Christ is subject to this prohibition.

The denial of bodily reality, then, is based on a new, different, and comprehensive understanding of reality, which stands under the imperative that the closed nature of the objective world must not be violated in any way: Miracles are impossible. The form of the this-worldly is inappropriate to express the reality of the other-worldly. In the last resort synthesis between them is materially impossible.[27]

Ott also notes the exclusiveness with which Bultmann is always saying "not . . . but." There is no *tertium quid*. Either-or, *tertium non datur*, is the controlling law in his program. Yet it might still be possible to regard one side as transcending and even overcoming the other, as the Old and New Testaments obviously believe.[28] But the subjection of the program to this either-or is not due to Bultmann's inability to think in any other way. It is due to the fact that the closed nature of the objective world, and consequently the antithesis between this world and the beyond, must not be violated, and yet the gospel must still be preached. Therefore the traditional message must be brought under the antithesis. *A third option, the "realization" of the other world in this world, would challenge the monopoly of the objective world, and is consequently unacceptable.*

In Ott's view, this twofold understanding of reality produces the two-layer anthropology according to which the bodily reality of man is to be distinguished and separated from the "history in which he really stands."[29] Hence, the site of God's work in the world is not to be defined in terms of time and space nor in terms of the bodily reality of man. God's work, too, must be non-objective. It cannot be localized, not even in the consciousness—for this, as Bultmann says in defense against Thielicke, is still a psychological phenomenon and thus objective.[30] Any element of world-relation or objectivity in anthropology must be kept out of statements about the reality of the world or work of God. Even *in* this world God's work has its locus *beyond* this world. To the degree that the world is man's world, God has nothing to do with it. And he has nothing to do with man to the degree that man is part of this world.

The invisibility and non-demonstrability of God's work

In the debate about the reality in which God works Bultmann has tried to buttress his position by arguing that God's work is *by nature* non-demonstrable. To human thought the offense of faith was precisely this non-demonstrability. Myth tried to evade this offense by speaking of visible, provable, objective phenomena. For Bultmann, then, his program of demythologizing is simply the execution of an already existing concern of faith.[31]

Bultmann deals with the matter very thoroughly. *His main axiom is that God's work cannot be seen or demonstrated in this world.* To speak of miracles as demonstrable processes is to reject the idea of God's hidden action. According to Bultmann, Paul was unfortunately doing this when he attempted to prove the resurrection of Jesus Christ from the dead (1 Cor. 15). Bultmann calls this a "dangerous" line of argument.[32] The "paradox of faith" is that it can interpret as God's act an event which is otherwise known in its natural and historical context. God's work in nature and history is as hidden for the believer as for anyone else. Authentic faith can say only that God acts in hidden fashion in this or that event.[33]

In the theology of demythologization, then, God's work is not to be thought of as a special work inserted in between secular events. It takes place *in* these events, and is indistinguishable from them. The seamless fabric of secular events which offers itself to the objective eye must not be broken.[34]

Plainly, Bultmann's argument is based on what is for him a dogma: God's work is unconditionally concealed, invisible. "The invisibility of God rules out every myth which tries to make him and his work visible."[35]

How does Bultmann support this claim to the hiddenness, invisibility, and non-demonstrability of the work of God which underlies the whole attempt to deobjectify God's work? He compares the non-objectivity of God's work to human love. Love cannot be apprehended by objective observation, he says, but only by the one affected by it. From the outside love is not visible; it may be "seen" only as a spiritual or psychological phenomenon subject to interpretation. He grants, of course, that the reality of love does not depend on whether it is understood or responded to.[36]

But if love is visible in its expression, if it becomes a "phenomenon" (as he admits), can these expressions be interpreted in so many different ways that they tell us nothing about the reality of love? One thing is certain: Love seeks to become objective. Third parties *can* see its work. Admitted, its phenomena may be interpreted in different ways. But can they ever be waived? And are they even that ambiguous? Is it not highly improbable, for example, that the love of the wife in Proverbs 31:12 is cold calculation rather than love?

We need not go into that here. It is enough that there is something objective, an act, a phenomenon and hence something tangible—and credible—even if it can still be taken in different ways. For if the act were not there, if love did not come to expression, it would be very hard to speak about the presence of love at all. In light of Bultmann's own illustration of self-expressive love, Paul's argument in 1 Cor. 15 is obviously not as "dangerous" as Bultmann would have us believe.

In fact the New Testament witnesses use the same reasoning about God's love to man as we have done about the love of the virtuous wife of Proverbs. John's Gospel says that God's love impels him to a decisive act: "For God so loved the world, that he gave his only Son . . ." (3:16). Love is not just a favorable disposition or a new understanding of man on God's part. Paul speaks no less plainly. Love is an inner movement that expresses, represents, and demonstrates itself in and by an act: "But God demonstrates his own love for us in this: While we were still sinners, Christ died for us" (Rom. 5:8).[37]

Love is indeed an excellent illustration of God's work; it leads us to seek its expression in objective reality. On the other hand, the illustration does not fit the program of demythologization, since it presupposes that (like any other inner movement of man!) love must express itself and become a secular phenomenon. Otherwise, it cannot even be perceived by the other person.

Possibly such terms as "demonstrable," "unequivocal," "affirmable," and "visible" belong to a different universe of meaning for Bultmann. Thus he says that wonders and ecstasies can be signs of the coming of the new age . . . but they cannot be proved unequivocally.[38] Fine—equivocal can stand for non-provable. But does it also mean invisible and hidden? God's work is not "provable" in the sense of being unequivocal or in the sense that its significance can be established beyond doubt. But equivocal does not mean invisible. We are speaking of events that are perceivable and yet can be interpreted in different ways.[39]

It may be assumed that Bultmann was led to the illustration of love by another element in his theology, his insistence on the "act of God" which is necessary to produce faith. But if this insistence is to mean anything it must refer to a phenomenon that is mediated through the senses and hence to something of the world. One of Bultmann's own phrases hints at the need for sensory (and therefore objective) impartation. He speaks at one point of the "sounding forth" of the Word of God.[40] If the object, God's act, does not consist only in the preaching of the contemporary preacher (Bultmann is unclear about this), it must be allowed that some objectivity still attaches to the work of God.

It is rather Bultmann's logical development of the closed picture of the objective world, imposed on him by his concept of myth, that leads him to the idea of the complete invisibility of God's work. Here, even *in contrast* to the phenomenon of human love, Bultmann insists that the person who wants to believe in God must realize that he has nothing which can serve as a basis for his faith, that he is left hanging in the air: "Security can be found only by abandoning all security, by being ready, as Luther put it, to plunge into the inner darkness."[41] Not only must man believe even though there is no basis for belief, but he can believe only contrary to appearances, through phenomena which seem to teach the opposite.[42]

This rounds off Bultmann's system. God can be believed in only and precisely against appearances, just as justification can be believed in only in spite of the accusations of conscience. *Hence Bultmann's radical demythologizing is supposed to be an epistemological parallel to Luther's doctrine of justification by faith without the works of the law.*[43] Such a generalization of the soteriological dogma in terms of epistemology logically implies a deistic God who produces no effects in this world. That he becomes man is now theologically, as well as ontologically, impossible. For its own sake, according to Bultmann, the gospel must speak of God's work contrary to all appearances. In order that faith may be true faith, nothing must be done by God's hand. God and his work must be invisible. Thus, demythologizing or deobjectifying is a requirement of faith itself.

Now obviously it is impossible to hold such a view of the Christian religion in order to endorse the "objective view of the world." One can even appeal to suitable dogmas, though this would clearly involve some loss of substance to the New Testament view. But the New Testament makes it clear that *the invisibility of God does not logically imply the invisibility of his work in the world.* On the contrary, the invisible God is proclaimed through his visible work, as is plain from the example of love. We see from this that observability and provability are two different things. An object can be present even though it can be interpreted in different ways. If it is there, one or the other interpretation can be right. If it is not, no interpretation is even possible. How far Bultmann's insistence on God's invisibility is a *philosophical* preconception may be seen in his statement that faith (that God calls me and works in me) can be grasped and held only in a *"nevertheless"* over against the world, for God and his acts *cannot* be visible in this world.[44]

"Detachment from the world" in the New Testament?

It is a remarkable fact that Bultmann thinks he represents Christianity in such statements.[45] But can we really understand the Bible rightly if we think it does not see or deal with any questions that refer to more than individual existence? Jesus agonized for the fate of a whole people: "O Jerusalem, Jerusalem . . . How often I have longed to gather your children together" (Matt. 23:37).

Bultmann does not base the question on existential philosophy alone, but argues that Heidegger's existential analysis of being is one and the same with the New Testament's own assessment of the essential features of human life, also in terms of detachment from the world and a renunciation of any attempt at shaping one's personality, society, or the world. "Everything in the world has become indifferent and unimportant."[46]

But is not the New Testament here being read already through the spectacles of existential analysis? Has not this analysis demanded such an interpretation from the very outset? This conclusion *must* be reached because shaping the world would also be a kind of objectification to be avoided from the very outset. But the New Testament view in fact seems to be in direct opposition to this. In the New

Testament the expressions of God's activity are plainly visible. They are *phaneros,* or evident.

DEOBJECTIFICATION: LOSS OF PRACTICE AND THE WORLD OF WORK

The program of deobjectification that follows from Bultmann's view of myth leads naturally to the thesis that corporeality, sociality, and the objective world have no meaning for Christian faith. Hence the program implies the surrender of practice and the world of human work into the hands of secularism. *Demythologizing affects the handling as well as the observing of reality.*

Man's existence in the world of work

Fritz Lieb, the social ethicist of Basel, has protested firmly against this division of reality and against a contempt of the world of objects through which the biblical kerygma suffers a monstrous reduction. Without the objective corporeality of historical events there can be no decision for or against God. God has created a space-time world, a bodily world. "How closely this hemmed the Saviour! How objective and tangible it was! God gave himself up to objectivity—the same objectivity that encloses, determines, and limits us whenever we work to build up our lives and the lives of our nations." According to the Scriptures, man has been given by God a specific sphere in which to demonstrate his divine likeness in Christ. The world of work is both the place of enslavement and the place of liberation, the place where the relation to God must be shaped aright. Is all this now meaningless, Lieb asks, just because Heidegger in his aristocratic prophecy has little interest in it?[47]

Where has evangelical theology been in past years that it has not listened to such a voice? Bultmann of course has had many Protestant allies and forerunners who reduced reality for faith. But a reduction that surrenders world phenomena and ignores corporeality and the psyche is new. This theology offers little stimulus or help in taking up a task for the world of men. But what was perhaps simply unfortunate neglect in nineteenth-century Christian romanticism is an actual requirement here. It is remarkable that for so long theology and the church have failed to see these aspects of Bultmann's venture. Lieb rightly points out that Feuerbach's charge against the Christianity of his day—which lacked corporeality and sociality—is fully justified against Bultmann's theology. In his wholly individualistic approach, the Christian faith threatens to become a purely private religion, indeed an opium to conceal from the people their true state.[48]

In this respect, Bultmann's theology may be compared to Bruno Bauer's philosophy of "pure thought" and "self consciousness" which the young Karl Marx fought against for the sake of a "realistic humanism": he was concerned not with man as "an abstract . . . encamped outside the world," but with "the world of man, the state, society."[49] The need to break with a philosophy (or a theology) of mere contemplation was plain enough from conditions in the working world of the time:

> . . . workers employed, for instance, in the Manchester or Lyons workshops, do not believe that by *"pure thinking"* they will be able to argue away their industrial masters and their own practical debasement. They are most painfully aware of the *difference* between *being* and *thinking,* between *consciousness* and *life.* They know that property, capital, money, wage-labour and the like are no ideal figments of the brain but very practical, very objective products of their self-estrangement and that therefore they must be abolished in a practical, objective way for man to become man not only in *thinking,* in *consciousness,* but in mass *being,* in life.[50]

The same principle applies to the bondage and liberation of man of which the gospel speaks. For man himself has to live objectively in an objective world. This is essential. He must also express himself in the world concretely. The young Marx learned this from the famous section on master and servant in Hegel's *Phenomenology of the Spirit.* It is man's nature to be active. In the theology of demythologization, however, his expressions or works do not belong to the nature and peculiarity of man. Bultmann suspends human existence in mid-air.

Autonomy and the ethical question

From Bultmann's cleavage between God's work and this world, from his incorporeality, individualism, and loss of practice, from the deobjectification of man and salvation, it follows that he should proclaim the autonomy of the world. And this he does in the closing arguments of his proposal. We have learned from Luther, he says, that there can be no holy places in the world. The whole world is profane in spite of the *terra ubique Domini.* For just as the justification of the sinner must be believed despite all appearances, so we must believe the rule of God despite the profane nature of the world. Only in the world of proclamation does what has happened and still happens in nature and history take on, for the believer, appearances to the contrary—the character of an act of God or a miracle. Specifically, for the believer, the world is profane and is restored to its own autonomy as the field of human work.[51] In short, according to Bultmann, *the world in which man lives—comprehensively described as the field of human work, nature, and history—is irrelevant for faith just as faith is irrelevant for this world.*

But from the thesis that evangelical faith can have no separate holy places, however, we must draw the opposite conclusion: the *whole* world stands under the demand of holiness. This is more in keeping with the proclamation of

Holy Scripture. Again, we cannot accept the thesis that the rule of God over the world is merely believed in contrary to appearances. Instead, the Christian consistently strives to alter the present evil state. The idea that the world must be restored to its own autonomy suggests that the world has hitherto been kept unjustly under the lordship of God. In this context, the words *profane* and *autonomy*, therefore, imply not merely a judgment about the nature of the world but also a judgment about God's lordship over it. The argument that God is not in this world and has no claim to it logically does away with the idea of the kingdom of God as has been well brought out by Buri, Lieb, and Ott.[52] The idea of the kingdom of God cannot be reconciled with the understanding of God's salvation as a mere change in individual self-understanding.

The phrase "field of human work" confirms our suspicions. As Bultmann intends, the whole sphere of human action is thereby given up to its own autonomy. This fits in with the view he expresses elsewhere that there is no Christian ethics any more than there is a Christian shoe factory.[53] Does this mean that our fellow-human is to be handled like a piece of leather, according to "autonomous" laws? After all, even in a shoe factory the question arises for whom shoes are made, and to answer this it is not enough to discuss the peculiarities of the material used. We must think of the people whose feet the shoes must fit. Again, can we equate construction laws with laws about working hours? Can materials and people be treated alike? There are glimpses here of an attitude that made possible the evils of early capitalism.

By what standards does man act in his field of work? We have to ask this, for the laws of nature offer only a specific framework within which he can manipulate and control nature. Is it a matter of indifference to Christians what laws rule over *man* in the field of human work?

If, as Bultmann avers, Christian life does not take place in shaping personality and human society, where then does it take place—and by what laws are personality and society shaped? What is done in this field by the man who calls himself a Christian elsewhere? For personality and society *will* be shaped if man is not an unchanging being. Man's intellectual life may for a moment be regarded as his essential world, and the message of the gospel may be applied to this. But then what about the working population which does not thus celebrate the intellectual life? And what about intellectual theologians when *they* work, associate, or act with their body?

In demythologization does Christianity end by just featuring the attitude of the individual to himself? But, as we have heard, not even his personality was to be shaped by himself. What, then, is Christian faith? Is it simply a way of looking at things, an insight, a standpoint, an additional act of interpreting the events that take place anyway in nature and history? Faith, according to the intentions of this program, is purely contemplative. Events that take place without it assume for the believer the character of being acts of God. They "become" this for him, as something is added in his view. But this is purely subjective. It is simply "for him." *The reality of the world remains the same in the face of faith.* The divine element is simply a way of looking at things. The final statement of Bultmann that, for the believer, the world "becomes profane" even contradicts the previous one, which does at least speak of God's rule over the world, appearances to the contrary. For we are now told that the appearances are right. The world actually is profane. This reduction of the gospel to a way of looking at things confirms the existing cleavage in Protestantism between theory and practice. Faith must maintain the exact opposite—the profanity of the world is an appearance that is false. In reality, the world is not profane. The Christian cannot be indifferent toward it.

What do New Testament ethics say to all this? The many

detailed admonitions in the New Testament do not fit in well at all with this system. New Testament Christianity has been and must be very active in shaping personality and human society; it relates to man's acts and to the social sphere in which he lives. The whole of the New Testament judges that man is summoned to a new walk and new conduct, not just to a new self-understanding. The old man is to be put off especially in terms of practice (Eph. 4:22). Both the old and the new man of which we read are no doubt invisible and "non-demonstrable," but their existence may be seen very plainly in conduct. *They are indeed so tangible in their works that the physical existence of man may depend on whether the old man or the new man comes to expression.* The point is that the new man must be objectified in actions.

This is why the New Testament puts love in the center. Love relates to the fellow-man. It proves: The reality in which God's work comes to light is in the dealings of man and man. It is an ethical, social, and historical reality. This love insists on objectifications. Paul organized a collection for the needy churches in Palestine. James rejected the attitude that when it sees others hungry and ill-clad, is content to say: "Go, I wish you well; keep warm and well-fed," without supplying what is needed (Jas. 2:16).

Bultmann's teaching impairs Christian action. Where there is already diaconal action out of a sense of duty, the program of demythologization shatters its theoretical basis, making the work of Christian love look accidental and capricious, so that it is finally stopped because it has no deeper meaning and authorization.

The program of deobjectification makes ethics pointless and leaves the world of objects without ethos or direction. In ethics, it proclaims atheism.

Deobjectification: the loss of history

Ethics and practice, the objective behavior of man in his

corporeality and sociality, are part of the reality of history. The apostles Paul and John have this reality in view when they say that the expressions, effects, and "phenomena" of the Holy Spirit must be found in reality.

But accepting history raises problems for the program of demythologization, since this is a program of deobjectification. In this program everything that takes place in nature and history is treated alike. Thus we are told that in general God is just as hidden in nature and history for the believer as he is for anyone else. The combination "nature and history" is a common one in Bultmann, as it is also in Braun who states that he is content to regard the this-worldly sphere as closed from the standpoint of natural law and history.[54]

This rolling-into-one of nature and history, in which both become meaningless for faith, cannot be justified. Just as we cannot uncritically adopt and accept the self-understanding of modern man, arbitrary and to be differentiated from the world picture of modern science, as Bultmann himself suggested, so we cannot believe that the sphere of history, in which man's self-understanding continually objectifies and actualizes itself and in which the human mind and will are thus at work, is an indifferent sphere. "If it is the inclusive claim of the sciences to discover reality," says C. F. von Weizsäcker, "then religion may press on with much the same degree of confidence."[55] Science can speak only about the *how* but not about the *why* in the world of human action. A broad field of values is necessary for the latter purpose. In the social sphere represented by history, human reason anyway does not reign alone. Human motives and evaluations also hold sway; there are irrationalities that we do not find in physics. Thus it seems to be a complete mistake to exempt the social and historical sphere from the criticism of the gospel and to declare it to be empty of values. This surrender reflects the mood of science at the beginning of the present century when scholarship was thought to lie outside the world of aims and values. *History is the same thing as the field of human work. The Christian cannot surrender it.*

The program of deobjectifying the gospel, however, has no interest in history and readily surrenders it. History is equated with non-human physical nature. This follows logically from the methodological cleavage of the New Testament kerygma into history and meaning. Under pressure of the "modern world view" Bultmann demands that the New Testament expression of the significance of the salvation event in cosmological categories (as in Col. 1) should be replaced by an expression in existential categories.[56]

Is there a reason, however, why Bultmann should start with cosmological statements and not with the historical event as the true content of proclamation? Does perhaps the whole enterprise rest on the fact that Bultmann understands the traditional object of theology as a cosmological one, as it mostly was in the philosophical theology of the last few centuries? Is the root to be seen in the fact that traditionally theology has been oriented more to cosmology than to social history?

In both the Old Testament and the New, however, history is more often than nature the sphere of God's work. The program of deobjectification, which begins with cosmology and leads to an existentialist ontology, bypasses history. Separating biblical history from its meaning, it thus defends a very different object from that which the Bible has in view. It should have sought God's work, and hence the traces of God's reality in world history, in the history of mankind and in the history of God's people. "Thy will be done, on earth as it is in heaven" (Matt. 6:10) points to a third sphere beyond myth and cosmological speculation on the one side, and beyond the new self-understanding and existentialist contemplativeness on the other. This third sphere is the sphere in which men live their real, everyday lives.

THE COLLAPSE OF BULTMANN'S POSITION

A highly abstract solution such as Bultmann's view of reality can last only a short time. Contradictions in it cry out for further elaboration; one cannot hang in the air too long. Theology reacts against the great lack of objectivity inherent in Bultmann's demythologizing program. Further development brings one more shift: an objective anthropology replaces a non-objective theology.

Such a reversal, derived from a human need for concreteness, seems to follow definite laws in the history of thought. We find similar steps in the collapse of Hegelianism. Hegel's philosophy contains a double christology. On the one hand, man in general—created man—is called the son of God. On the other hand, the one Jesus of Nazareth, as in the Christian confessions, is the Son of God, the Messiah. Soon after Hegel's death, what was previously thought to be the supreme synthesis of wisdom now seemed to demand decision. Hegel's followers wanted rationality, and they had to choose. D. F. Strauss denied that the fullness of wisdom could appear and take concrete form in a single man. Instead, he sought it in the abstract category of the *species* of man. Hegel's ambiguity was ended. But then there was a further need to get back from abstraction to the concrete world. Strauss did this by substituting the sociological entity of humanity for the species man. But this again was still inadequate, and Feuerbach carried the process further by seeking and proclaiming the fullness of truth and the human in the smallest representation of the whole, the fellowship of the I and the Thou. The tangible reality of the everyday world was finally reached.

The followers of Bultmann seem to have taken a similar way back to objectivity and tangible fellowship, although now without the "act of God" on which Bultmann insisted.

In his book *The New Man*, Ronald Gregor Smith, translator of Bultmann (and Buber), anticipated much of what

Bishop Robinson was to say later in his famed *Honest to God*. Robinson himself called Smith a pioneer in the new development.[57] Smith found in Bultmann's work a solution to the problem of the diastasis of church and culture. Showing Bultmann's influence on him, he called God's entry into the reality of the world, not an extra added to history, but the other side of one and the same situation. His recurrent formula was the demand for a "this-worldly transcendence."[58] The experience of transcendence is now to be located in commitment to others as exemplified by Jesus. It thus follows that encounter with God is always in and through, rather than apart from or in addition to, encounter with men.[59] Smith thus restored concreteness to Bultmann's vague "act of God," although Bultmann himself had tended to find a new place for the salvation event in the encounter with the preacher of the Word. At any rate, for Smith, God is transcendence in the event of fellow-humanity.

We find something similar in Braun. In his proposals we constantly detect the freshness and liveliness of a new concreteness, the rediscovered natural naïveté of real man. To Bultmann's non-objective theology he opposes a new anthropology. In antithesis to Bultmann he even expresses interest in the pre-Easter life of Jesus, the *what* rather than the *that,* indeed in the what *apart* from the that, a timeless anthropological content. For Braun, God does not act in a vacuum. He presupposes, of course, that the elements of time and objectivity in the biblical accounts of God's acts don't make sense for us.[60] They are an "inadequate objectification."[61] This means, then, that there must be such a thing as an adequate objectification, even though this is no longer historical. Indeed, God is "where I am committed . . . man as man, man in fellow-humanity."

Smith and Braun are evidence that Gollwitzer was right: Bultmann's position is *transitional*. We can tarry only for a moment at this extreme, in this contradictoriness of events.

Then the immanent contradictions force us to move on to full dekerygmatization in which there is no longer any reference to the "once for all," to the proper name of Jesus, to the "act of God" in Christ, and in which it is no longer possible to see — for this would also be a compromise — how Jesus is to be more than an example.

The question must arise whether Feuerbach, the pronounced atheist, perhaps understood Christianity correctly after all. Feuerbach stands at the end of this development. Thus Braun, unlike his teacher, not only does not hold aloof from the atheism of Feuerbach's logic, but he comes very close to Feuerbach positively when he seeks and finds the essence of religion not in the self-exposition of man, as did Bultmann, but in "exposition in encounter,"[62] in fellow-humanity, exactly as did Feuerbach. The plain result of demythologization, and the only possibility for development of this program after Bultmann, is that Feuerbach is the true prophet, his humanistic atheism the true understanding of Christianity.[63]

The only other option is that, once the prejudices and illogicalities of the program are perceived, "the doors Bultmann has closed should be carefully and individually opened again" (Ott),[64] and that his negations and hasty erasures will be corrected. But this will mean turning round and leaving the path blazed by Bultmann's program.

Results

Bultmann expected it would take a whole a generation of theologians to solve the problem he had posed. In effect, he at least decisively influenced the thinking of a whole generation of theologians. We welcome his confessed aim of declaring the gospel in such a way that modern man can come back to a relationship with God. Much preaching in the church has become abstract and unintelligible. Hence an effort must be made to bring the Christian message to the modern age in a new way and to set theology and the church, which have become alienated from reality, back on the ground of everyday life and speech. Bultmann's declared intention should be respected and adopted.

Yet we must bring the following criticisms against his attempt to achieve the goal.

(1) The demythologization program subjects the gospel to alien judgments of existence, to investigations restricted by philosophical influences and to implicitly alien value judgments. It is as impossible to hold to both a "closed world" and the "act of God" as it is to square a circle. Demythologization thus brings the Christian faith into insoluble self-contradiction. It also opens up an era of allegorizing that one might have thought to be impossible after decades of critical biblical research.

(2) The demythologization program has deobjectified the reality of God's saving work and hence destroyed it for man, whose existence is by its very nature objective. The development of a Death-of-God-theology, the transition from dubious theism to simple atheism, from the sorry complications for Bultmann's concept of God to the uncomplicated serenity of quasi-religious humanism, is an unavoidable consequence. To declare God's unreality, to confess him only as a concept, is already more than semi-atheism. Just as in ethics, changes in moral practice at once produce a demand for corresponding changes in hitherto accepted norms, so the same thing happens in the doctrine of God. It is as if we would finally call the child by his name and give the right name to a reality without God. Atheism in practice will become atheism in principle and concept.

The demythologization program tacitly erases as well the personal relationship to God. It makes it unthinkable. This is an inescapable consequence when the Other One is made an abstraction which can be held only with inner contradictions.

Proof may be found in the shady character of prayer in the new theology. Prayer is consistently reduced to meditation—man conversing with himself. In keeping with this is the proposition within the milieu of demythologizing that it makes no sense to talk of loving God. We are supposed to know *that* God has acted. But we cannot know *who* God is or *what* he has done. Can I love an unknown God?

Perhaps this is the reason why the piety of this theology, unlike Barth's, is so lacking in joy. "If you loved me, you would have rejoiced" (John 14:28). Any theology that does not help us to love God is ultimately worthless. Not for nothing does a New Testament theologian say that to love Christ is better than all knowledge (Eph. 3:19), for it is a general truth that "knowledge puffs up, but love builds up" (1 Cor. 8:1).

This concept of the unknowability of God has far-reaching implications; our gratitude toward God is also affected. Can we experience gratitude when we know next to nothing about the one who supposedly has acted toward us? But without gratitude, there can be no zeal for doing good in the Christian life.

(3) This leads us to the decisive criticism. If theology teaches us that God has nothing to do with man's world, then man must consciously shape his world atheistically, without God. If the world is not to be shaped in a Christian way, then it must be shaped in a non-Christian way.

With its proclamation of the "autonomy" of the world of work, the demythologization program systematically rounds off its practical atheism. Inevitable ethical consequences correspond to the ontological statements about the reality, or unreality, of God's work in the world. Denial of God's operation in nature and history is accompanied by denial of his claim to lordship over man, who shapes the world. This confirms what we suspected at the outset in relation to the existential character of atheism. *At root, atheism is not a denial of God's existence. It is a denial of his lordship.* The greatest fault in the demythologization program is that it allows secular thought to make this denial, that it backs the denial and even offers a justification for it. The program opens the door to atheism in ethics. It adds unconditional practical atheism to its conditional theoretical atheism.

With the conceptuality of a truncated view of man that results from the concept of "self-understanding," with the cleavage of reality, with the exclusive principle of believing in spite of appearances, with the surrender of the world and history to its own autonomy, with the thesis that New Testament Christianity is to be understood essentially as detachment from the world, Bultmann has put a wedge between Christianity and the formation of the world. Above all others in this century, he has made Christianity a private affair.[65] He has proclaimed the self-exclusion of Christianity from society and public life. Without a struggle he has abandoned the vast field of human labor. He has worked out reasons and explanations for this step. Naturally, other ideas and theories stream into the intellectual vacuum this leaves, and they bode little that is good for man.

There have been models for this decision and its consequences in the history of Christianity. The English historian and economist R. H. Tawney has described in devastating detail the abdication of the church from the area of economics and social theory.[66] Under the ideological pressure of the spirit of the eighteenth century, the church abandoned this field and thus opened the way to the abuses of the early factory system from whose results and reactions we are still suffering in world politics today. The acquiescence of the Lutheran Reformation in the horrors of National Socialism also had been predetermined long before. There again a theology and church had conceded that business and politics are no concern of religion.

Bultmann peddles that program today, and history might repeat itself. For this reason we must resist any declaration that the Christian faith has nothing to say about the objective reality of human life. The demythologization program is not a new version of the gospel of Jesus Christ, but a way into the wilderness.

3

A DETERIORATION OF THE DOCTRINE OF GOD:

Barth and the Unreality of God in the World

TOWARD THE END OF 1963, I talked with Barth about the latest developments in church and theology. John A. T. Robinson's notorious book, *Honest to God,* after enjoying great success in England, had just been brought out in a German translation by the very house that had published Barth's own books before his expulsion from Hitler's Germany. This press, which had been generally regarded as a platform for Barthians, was now helping to spread the very theology Barth had been opposing most of his life.

During the conversation Barth said, "I often think the problem of John Robinson is more a problem of Karl Barth. What have I done wrong that this is now possible again — the force and breadth of this reaction? That the church today is in a condition in which it can absorb three hundred thousand copies of this book as a dry sponge sucks in water?"

These words of Barth show something of his true

greatness. They point to the humility with which, as a theologian, he recognized his own responsibility for the way taken by the church to which he belonged and which he served. This is humility, not arrogance. High regard for Barth should not prevent us, however, from pursuing the question Barth himself raised. It may be a painful question, but it is a necessary one. For there develops in some of Barth's work, although one may not expect it from him, a deterioration of the doctrine of God that is not dissimilar to that discussed under the name of Bultmann.

The Unreality of Salvation in the Early Theology of Barth

Barth and Bultmann: the same point of departure

The Enlightenment's veto of any transition from the other world to this world or vice versa can be overridden in other ways than that attempted by Bultmann. Barth makes his own different attempt. But he shares a common starting point with Bultmann in that both seem to adopt the presuppositions of secularism.

Let us compare the philosophical presuppositions of the modern world, which Bultmann advances, to radar equipment. Enemy aircraft may evade this radar by flying almost at ground level—the level of this-worldliness—so that, as in Bultmann, the main concern is to stay as low as possible while remaining aloft. But Bultmann fails to stay aloft.

The other way to avoid the radar scan is to fly higher than the radar's capacity. In this case, flight continues securely and unhindered, but without contact with the ground (reality). What we have now is escape into transcendence—the level of other-worldliness—about which, according to Kant, nothing can be proved or disproved. This is Barth's attempt. His theology, too, is thus a deobjectification of theological statements and a surrender of this-worldly reality, transferring the content of biblical statements into the supraterrestrial and suprahistorical world of transcendence. He flies above the radar. What is, as far as I know, the first Marxist examination of modern Protestant theology describes the theology of Karl Barth as an attempt to evade the demands of secularism in just this way.[1]

The first two chapters of our study brought to light the theme of the unreality of God through a study of Bultmann's program. In this chapter, I will not attempt a full treatment of even this one aspect of Barth's theology, but simply describe some symptoms of the same disease also to be found here and there in his theology.

Overcoming historicism was the basic issue for Barth, as it was for Bultmann. Barth only took a different path.[2] Both began with the question forced on theology by positivist historicism (the radical relativizing of all traditions previously regarded as inviolable).[3] Both were students of the Marburg theologian Wilhelm Herrmann, who taught them that the non-demonstrability of faith with respect to its object was actually its strength. Their common orientation may be illustrated by the following characteristic quotations.

Already in 1928 Bultmann used the term *life* in the Gospel of John to describe the other-worldliness and transcendence of the divine action. The character of this life is perfectly plain: "As the presence of the historical Jesus does not lie in historical effects and historical reconstruction, as it cannot be demonstrated in the present or in the past, but is his presence in the authorized Word, so life is not something demonstrable or there; neither is it inwardness or experience."[4]

Barth speaks similarly in his commentary on Romans. Redemption is the non-observable, the impossible, the inaccessible. It meets us only as a hope, as knowledge. It is not a divine facticity that can be seen. It is not objectivity. There is no such thing as the intrusion of that kingdom into this world.[5] There is nothing here to experience, to analyze, or to tell. In the same vein, in 1934, Barth insisted that Luther never thought he could display this new luster in his heart, which his hymns sing about, in human conditions and relations.[6]

The invisibility of God's work

The second edition of Barth's *Romans* really could teach a person the pathos of deobjectification. This comes through so clearly that even Bultmann, in his review, was uneasy: "Nothing demonstrable or there; not inwardness or experience." About this main work of the early Barth, Bultmann reports that for Barth faith was not visible for psychological observation. It was a blank or a "vacuum." It was the same, of course, for historical science to the extent that it seeks to describe the observable reality of human life in time.[7]

The investigations of historicism and psychologism must be halted once and for all, according to Barth. Neither God nor his works are to be found in the observable reality of human life in time. That is also where theology must no longer look. Faith can claim no historical or psychological reality, for it is "the inexpressible reality" of God.[8] The observable reality of human life in time and "the inexpressible reality" of God are set in antithesis. And if the theological ox does not want to go through the new gate of the non-observability of God's work, this stick can coax it through: "Religious experience . . . in its historicity, facticity, and concreteness is always a betrayal of God."[9]

This puts it rather daringly in view of the many witnesses to God's acts in history, as we find these in the Old and New Testaments. To speak of a "betrayal of God" in the face of the "historicity, facticity, and concreteness" of the child in the crib at Bethlehem "when Cyrenius was governor of Syria" seems to be a trifle pert. For in the manger we after all do have an "observable reality of human life in time." But as Bultmann suggested in his review, Barth's outburst must be viewed as the sharp reaction against a liberal theology that used to set man and his religious experiences at the center of the stage: "It is evident that this radicalism, which does not fear paradox and even the appearance of blasphemy, is simply trying to express the fact that faith or justification is an absolute miracle. But is not the paradox overdone?" Bultmann gave precision to this question when he put it in a form that could later be turned against his own program, "Is faith anything real at all if it is sundered from every process of the soul and if it is *beyond consciousness?*"[10]

The one-sided exaggeration with which Barth in the second edition of *Romans* put all the emphasis of theological statements on transcendence began with an incisive expository stroke. Barth translated *pistis theou*, normally understood as man's faith in God, as "faithfulness of God." A statement about *man's* believing becomes, through his daring translation, a statement about *God's* faithfulness. Technically speaking, *fides qua* becomes *fides quae:* The attitude of faith is absorbed into faith's object and the emphasis on a human action is removed. The New Testament scholar A. Jülicher protested strongly against this in his review of the book. Careful exegete that he was, Bultmann, despite his theological affinity to Barth, could not let Barth's dogmatic horses leap over the hedge of the text in this way. "At the very least," he said, Barth's exposition is "not the meaning of Paul": In Paul a distinction was made between justification and faith. Justification was God's supratemporal act on man, but faith was the paradoxical fact of the *appropriation* of this act of God in the consciousness of man, and indeed of the individual man. Bultmann closed his review with an excellent statement which again, as it were, criticizes in advance his own later view. Faith is not a "pseudo-transcendent factor," he said. "My faith is a determination of my consciousness. This means that faith cannot exist without confession. It seems to me, however, that Barth does not do justice to faith as confession."[11]

Confession—man's appropriation of that non-observable, inexpressible event of justification—requires at least a perceptible utterance by man, a word or an act. This corresponds to the train of thought in Romans. Paul follows up the great passage on the appropriation of salvation by man in Romans 6:1-10 by speaking of the service of righteousness which is to take place through the concrete and by no means "non-observable" medium of the "members" of man. Through these the invisible event of justification is activated in reality, in the world of corporeality.

But Barth does not want that. Instead, we find him defending the principle of the non-observability of God's work (which follows from the systematic development of his axiom, the "infinite qualitative distinction between God and man") even against the force of concreteness in the text of Paul. In his exposition of Romans 6, he maintains the non-observability of the salvation event, thus preceding Bultmann's program of deobjectification of 1928 on both counts: for Barth the resurrection of Jesus is not an event of historical extension like the other events of Jesus' life and death. Nor is my walk in newness of life, which impresses itself upon me as a necessity and reality in the power of the resurrection, an event like other events. The "I" which is created anew in Christ is hid with Christ in God (Col. 3:3); the new is merely an invisible viewpoint and point of relation. Non-temporal and non-observable, it lies beyond all the temporal and observable events of my life.[12]

Plainly, Barth is concerned solely with what lies beyond the reality described as world, time, and man. The new life, the effect of justification, has such little reality that Barth can denote it only by the verbs may, can, ought, and will. As these verbs painfully indicate, the new life is still to come, strictly "eschatological." In *this* life, nothing changes except that we acquire an invisible viewpoint.[13]

When Barth comes to Paul's statements about the logical outworking of the new life in the sphere of the "members"

(Rom. 6:11f), one would think he could hardly avoid describing the observable, concrete reality of human life and action. And in fact we do read now of a new *being, having* and *doing* that correspond to the "Christ in us." Finally, we are indeed permitted to see with our eyes and hear with our ears the *revelation* and *observation* of the ineffable grace of God. In immediate proximity to the systematic principle of the non-observability of God's work, Barth now concedes freely that grace cannot be silent, despite the iron curtain separating the non-observable from the observable, the infinite from the finite.[14]

However, we should not rejoice too soon. These liberating statements that expound Romans 6:19 are soon relativized back to the level of *may, can, ought,* and *will*. Grace *wills* all that has been said. New being, life, and action are indeed "demanded." Grace "reaches out," "attacks," and "demands." It at least questions what we are doing. Following naturally from Barth's principle of non-observability, however, is the adversative, but: (this possibility is—a phrase Barth cherishes—the possibility of the impossible. Hence, not merely the new life itself, but also its manifestation in the members, is finally an event of the future. It takes place only on the new earth and in the new heaven.[15] In the present reality of man's life, everything is still demand, the mere wish of God's grace. The work of God in the justification of the sinner achieves only the quasi-reality of "as though": "As though sin did not dwell in your mortal body."[16]

Thus, even in face of the concrete conclusions of Paul, Barth everywhere maintains the non-observability and unreality of God's work in man and of man's work. "God is in heaven and thou on earth"—this methodological principle of Barth's *Romans* forces a sharp cleavage between God's reality and man's reality, just as in Bultmann's program of demythologization. Here too, man's bodily reality is to be differentiated from the "history in which he really stands."

For both Barth and Bultmann, the question arises whether there is even a place for the practical outworking of faith, for "members" to be "instruments of righteousness."

The question of the possibility of ethics

Is an ethics possible within a system such as Barth's? The cleavage of reality into a reality of God and a reality of the world might imply that there can be no human action that in any way would relate to the reality of God. This implication was soon noticed. In I. Rilliet's view of Barth, "Gnosis replaces faith, and an indifference which is very dangerous in practice replaces ethics."[17] This indifferent gnosis is illustrated when Barth even eschatologizes Paul's admonition to put on the whole armor of God (Eph. 6:10-17). He relegates the putting on of this armor to the final conflict in the last day, categorically asserting that no human virtues and acts are at issue here. The whole armor, he says, is not under our control. "The invitation to put it on is not a call for inner depth, enrichment, purification, or amendment; nor is it a demand for specific attitudes or acts," and "most certainly not in the sense of a moral re-armament." But how, then, can we "put it on"? What does Paul have in mind? The answer for Barth can only be a cheerful confession and a cheerful faith—confessing with the lips and believing in the heart. "We neither may nor should do anything new or special." We are simply to continue the confession of the lips and the faith of the heart.[18]

But what, then, of that new and special work of love, of which Jesus said that "wherever this gospel is preached in the whole world, what this woman has done shall also be spoken of in memory of her" (Matt. 26:13)? Quite apart from his exegetical daredeviltry, Barth's words suggest that ethical concreteness alongside faith is actually *forbidden*. Of the totality of members Paul wanted mobilized, it seems that the heart and lips alone have a place in the present service of Christ and warfare of the Christian.

In his discussion of the Christian's armor, Barth actually expands his argument that *pistis theou* is not an attitude of man, but faithfulness as a quality of God: With reference to truth, righteousness, readiness for the gospel, love and faith, he now says that God does all these and is all these! *We thus find a process of reduction, as in Bultmann, except that now all statements about man are changed into statements about God, and not vice versa as in Bultmann.* If Gollwitzer could say about Bultmann's program that the subject (God) was in danger of being swallowed up by the predicates, the opposite danger exists for Barth: the predicates can all be swallowed up by the subject. In both cases an impermeable wall exists between this world and the other, and the living relationship between God and man is lost. The difference is that for Bultmann "reality" is only in *this* world, while in Barth it is only in the beyond. In the former we have only man's work; in the latter, only God's. Both respect an iron curtain between God and man, and both make one side empty, finally abandoning it to demons. In this regard, the crucial statement of Barth's dates from 1923: "No objectivity . . . no grasping of man and no coming of that kingdom into this world." This was the basis—with the result that, "not knowing God or his kingdom, knowing only the sighing of all creation, we may agree with any honest secular view of nature and history, but never with the 'superficialities' of a theological view of nature and history."[19] Under heaven man is to do the best he can with his own wisdom—or with that of his secular neighbor!

The upshot for theology, and especially for ethics, is obvious. What Barth said of Hermann Kohlbrügge, the nineteenth century Dutch divine in whose vestiges he walked, applies equally to his own early theology: namely, that there is a danger that obedience will disappear in faith, the grace of sanctification in the grace of justification, and the law in the gospel. Nor can it be denied that this has sometimes happened among Kohlbrügge's followers.[20]

The unreality of God's saving work in early Barthianism

Barth's salvation objectivism—the doctrine of the non-observability of God's work and the elimination of concreteness from theology—dominated theology for thirty years. The question of the appropriation and working out of justification *in* and *by* man was largely ignored. Among some of Barth's followers, it disappeared altogether. During the period of Barth's supremacy, one finds dissertations on the new creation and the new birth which, after the manner of Kohlbrügge and Barth, claim that the new birth of man took place exclusively at Golgotha. The question of the reality of the new creation in man's life is briefly raised and then dismissed. In a title like "The Reality of Salvation in Paul" the word "reality" is at once put in quotations: Grace is no ordinary "reality"; it is not concrete, observable, or objective—it is the "divine fullness of life." For death claims our visible reality.[21] (Question: Is the divine fullness of life then abstract on principle?) For these Barthians, the reality of the new life becomes objective and observable only in eschatological consummation.[22] In this kind of total eschatologizing, renewal disappears into justification and even the "Christ in us" is solely explained as "Christ for us" (and outside us!). No experience or psychological manifestation! The supreme reality is hidden, non-objective, not "compromised by manifestation in time."[23]

The effects of salvation are all hidden in a metaphysical beyond. "Being led by the Spirit"—there are no marks of this. But what is not actually there, what is not experienced, is to be *believed*. "Dying and rising again with Christ" (Gal. 2, Phil. 3) refers to no actual process in a person's life. Even "daily dying with Christ," for Paul something *experienced* in the old body in suffering and persecution, is now merely "believed."

How young theologians were tossed about between the clear statements of the New Testament and the authority of theological opinion may be seen from K. Mittring's handling of Romans 6. Being "raised with Christ" is not the same as an objective moral and religious renewal. (We finally see here the real stumbling stone. Rejected along with objectivity is the demand for a moral and religious renewal.) *But* it does have some presence in the visible form of life, too.[24] While on the one hand "the situation has nothing to do with the objectivity of a moral renewal or vital change," on the other hand in Romans 6:11f. we come up against the "existential necessity of standing at God's disposal with our members and our visible life."[25]

In another young theologian at the time, whose heading "The Hiddenness of Reality" was dictated by the theological spirit of the age, we find the same conflict with the plain statements of the New Testament: "Man gains a new existence through Christ, but he cannot manifest this newness in the 'objective' phenomena of his present life. The knowledge that he is new is a knowledge of *faith. Nevertheless,* within the Christian life and especially the community there are *phenomena* that *seem* to represent the renewal visibly, that seem to objectify the Spirit. There is the suffering of the Apostle. But this is always a broken judgment."[26]

That certain "phenomena"—which *are* there but should *not* be there—must lead only to a "broken judgment" is an indication of the contradictions into which a whole generation of theologians—and exegetes especially—was flung by the domination of Barth's early theology. It is no surprise that so imperious a rule was all the more quickly shaken off when the time came.

When theologians disowned the sphere of the practice and the psychology of new life, secular theories soon took over. A Swiss pastor and a member of Barth's movement once flatly told me that, on the basis of the purely eschatological exposition of the Sermon on the Mount by Eduard Thurneysen (Barth's close friend and a main proponent of Barth's objectivism) he had rejected the perceptibility of the work of faith and thus thrown out the New Testament idea of "fruits." He claimed that there could be no such thing. He could then accept the presupposition of a social or psychological determinism: Paul's total commitment as seen from Phil. 3:7f. was due to purely natural causes; "others are constitutionally incapable of the same phenomenon." That is the other side of the deobjectification of God in the world: the surrendering of the world of objectivity. Still today, Barth's theology is praised by some for this particular tendency, for example by the so-called theology of revolution. Thus, Richard Shaull has said that the work of Barth, with its emphasis on the otherness of God and of the Word of God standing over against all human thought and achievement, "has given us an astonishing new freedom in relation to culture and society."[27] It is the freedom to submit to secularist presuppositions.

THE AMBIVALENCE OF BARTH'S THEOLOGY

The paradox of political ethics

But are we construing Barth aright in relation to his doctrine of the transcendence of God and the resultant indifference to ethics? Barth has certainly never said, as Bultmann has, that Christianity has nothing to do with shaping the world. On the contrary, each section of his later *Church Dogmatics* has its own chapter on ethics, and Barth himself was constantly making very visible political decisions. But could not the Mozartian cheerfulness which Barth recommended because, despite earthly events, God was ruling on his throne anyway, make a serious word from the theologians about that earthly reality practically unnecessary?

In fact both attitudes may be seen in Barth: The dilemma of total commitment to the *other* world and necessary decision in *this* world can be expressed in one and the same essay by Barth. In face of, for example, the martial boasting of National Socialism, Barth can say that the Christian is one who, with uplifted head, marches on to the *ultimate* decision. But then he concludes that "no one can refuse to take sides today or avoid the *penultimate* decision required of us." This is a far cry from the spirit of his *Romans* of almost twenty years earlier, which suggested that the Christian does not get entangled in penultimate decisions. In the same essay of 1940, Barth even added that like the Finns, in their defense against attack by the Soviet Union, we have "to pray and to work—to work too, which in this case unfortunately means to shoot."[28] The paradox is surprising. Earlier Barth forbade anything new or special; action seemed to have no place at all except in faith and confession; God did all the working. But now he requires so tangible a thing as shooting. How are we to explain this conflict?

One possibility is that, as some have emphasized, Barth, for example, already had a party loyalty as a socialist, even before he began to develop his theological system. The Marxist observer Milan Machovec gets this impression. Thus Barth's active participation in politics, Machovec suggests, is a historical accident, not a logical part of his theology, at least not of dialectical theology; Barth's political activism is a presupposition, not a conclusion.[29]

But a second explanation seems to be closer to the facts. Barth indeed demanded that the decision to confess Jesus Christ should never be apart from time, space, and body and without the form, sound, and color of the specific decisions that today agitate the church and the world.[30] How little this demand is required by his own starting point, however, may be seen from his exposition of Philippians 3. If faith as a determinant of human action is left as empty as possible and the whole stress is laid upon God— the ground of faith—how is it (Barth himself asks) that when Paul speaks of a battle for the righteousness of God he has such a liking for the metaphor of the race in the arena? One would not have expected this. He who knows only righteousness from God (knows God only as the subject of faith, never as the object of faith) ought to know only a life of inaction. But Paul knew nothing of this; he knew only a life in supreme, even frenzied, activity.[31] Such a paradox must arise for Barth because of his exegetical change from faith as exercised by man (in order to appropriate God's gift of righteousness) to faith as the faithfulness of God. It is this mistaken presupposition that turns concreteness, missionary effort, Paul's liking for the metaphor of the race, and ethics into *unexpected* implications.

At the same time we also see here the answer to the enigma of how Barth after all does link dogmatics and ethics, God's action and man's. Barth is not so stubborn about his methodological presuppositions that he can no longer see the evidence and logic of the *Bible*. He accepts it even when its ethics contradict his own dogmatic presupposition. In other words, Barth is a theologian who reads Scripture; because of this, his initial onesidedness leads at least to paradox. But a paradox remains, generated by the broken link between dogmatics and ethics. Human action appears to be accidental, not following logically from his dogmatics both in terms of its motivation and in relation to the content of actual decision. Barth's politics never completely lost this appearance of contingency.

This paradoxical character of Barth's theology is Machovec's starting point for his own proposal to develop Barth's theology in the direction of Marxism. It is natural, he says, that a conception like Barth's which is very logical and consistent in form but often self-contradictory in

content (especially in social implications), demands immediately to be thought through to the end. In Barth himself,
however, there is a contradiction. On the one hand, Machovec suggests, there is approximation practical to atheism
or socialism, while on the other there is devotion to the
traditional, fideistic, and miraculous side of Christianity.
The two aspects are not convincingly adjusted.[32] Ambivalence in relation to practice, if not a tendency to abstraction
and pure theory, is present at any rate in the early stages of
Barth's theology. Machovec thinks that is proven by the fact
that Barth later was aware that in many of his works he had
given the impression that theology should be neutral in
secular conflicts. But when he noted that neutrality encouraged the negative forces, and that ground can never be given
in the regulation of human conduct without other powers
taking over the territory, he began to exert himself to show
especially that dialectical theology should not be interpreted in terms of defeatism, fatalism, or a spirit of
capitulation.[33]

The principle of analogy

In his later *Church Dogmatics*, Barth attempted to reunite
the other world and this world, God and the world, without
in any way weakening the absolute precedence of God with
which he started. He sought to link the two worlds by the
concept of analogy.

What is at issue here? Barth had earlier dismissed the
principle of the analogy-of-being in Roman Catholic theology as the work of the devil. That a picture or concept of
God could be developed out of the phenomena, magnitudes, or attributes of this world was, for him, impossible.
This type of theology had been his constant target — "religion" that was in reality atheism. It was exactly the theology
that Feuerbach (with Barth's subsequent approval) had so
effectively demolished. But now Barth himself found the

solution to the problem through analogy—however, an analogy that was reversed. We are to move not from secular magnitudes, movements, and relationships to God, but from magnitudes, movements, and relationships in God to the world and man. In distinction from the Scholastic "analogy of being," Barth called this the "analogy of faith." The relation of the original and the copy is now turned upside down. What was previously the *analogans,* the starting point, the world and man, is now the *analogatum.* The original is above and the copy or image below.[34]

However, the unfortunate elements of idealism and other-worldly orientation in Barth's early theology have not been entirely corrected by this principle of analogy. If an element of Platonism had been detected earlier in Barth's work, it was even more strongly developed by the principle of analogy from the above downward, for this principle runs through Platonism. Barth wrote about his rendering of the biblical doctrine of creation that "a supreme Platonism can suddenly become the (apparently unavoidable and in this sense adequate) medium of expression."[35]

The criticism of Plato's view of reality by the young Marx may be applied with almost as much justice to Barth's new analogical conception of this world and the beyond: "Plato's views . . . his relation to reality in such a way that an independent realm of ideas about reality . . . hovers beyond it and is obscurely reflected in it." The natural result is that determination, articulation, and movement are banished from this world.[36] This description might not inappropriately be applied to Barth's new conception of this world.

Barth's concept of reality

The principle of analogy, as one may see from the Marx quotation, raises at once the question of Barth's relation to reality. If there are two spheres of being, the this-worldly and the transcendent, related respectively as copy and original, the title of reality seems to belong strictly only to the second.

Barth struggles with reality from the very first. For him, it is always a question how we can manage it, and how it may be seized or gotten rid of. The early works of Barth often describe it as the evil reality that will be done away with in God's future: He speaks of the oozing away of the ocean of reality that now washes over the island of truth, for the things that are seen are temporal (2 Cor. 4:18). Thus what is not hope is a block or fetter, heavy and sharp, like the word reality. It does not set free but imprisons. It is not God but a reflection of unredeemed man.[37] Hope and reality are unrelated. Reality imprisons man. It seems to be invincibly opposed to God's word. There is no sound of the weapons of our warfare that are strong enough through God for pulling down strongholds that . . . oppose the knowledge of God, or to bring reason to obedience to Christ (2 Cor. 10:5). For Barth in *Romans* God and reality cannot be related or united. They belong to two different sides: "God is in heaven and thou art on earth."[38] Of course, the Platonism of this pessimistic solution does not fit in with the biblical testimony that the Word was made flesh and that God himself became human and historical reality. But then, one tries to get away with a cleavage in one's concept of reality.

There are thus two realities—this and that. To the reality that is "block and fetter" belongs the existence of a Jesus of Nazareth, if he may be known historically, although that is of little interest. It is no surprise that Barth—like Bultmann and his school later on—uses 2 Corinthians 5:16 as a systematic basis for his lack of interest in history and its reality. Barth too already used the arbitrary trick of distinguishing between historic (*geschichtlich*) and historical (*historisch*). What "human" is—whether "historic" or "historical," this reality or that—he does not say. At this point, Barth is not far from the concept of reality Bultmann espoused when he distinguished between purely worldly phenomena and "the history in which we really stand."

The doctrine of the Incarnation, however, makes it necessary that a new concept of reality be found. This new concept of reality is the one where the Incarnation can then be located, yet without bearing the burden of ordinary reality or dashing its foot against the stone of objectivity. This new, second concept of reality dominates vast stretches of Karl Barth's *Church Dogmatics*.

The concept of reality is central, for instance, to Barth's doctrine of man. The "real" man of Barth's anthropology is identical with what is usually called true or essential man. "Real" man is *realized* man—not empirical, concrete man as we meet him every day in the newspaper, or as we ourselves are in real life. For Barth, the "very man" of the creed is "real" man.

When Barth was teaching in Basel, the biologist Adolf Portmann was also there, giving excellent lectures on biological and philosophical anthropology. Barth actually quoted his books in the *Church Dogmatics*. But does not the theologian as he analogizes from above to below already know everything about real man before the biologist can even open his mouth? When Barth spoke of the "phenomena of the human," he did not mean "real" man in the sense of what he called a "serious theological anthropology." Barth's theological anthropology did not wrestle with the elements of the human that are before us every day. It deals with "what God knows of man." It is a statement of faith. What it says about man stands within a bracket before which we read: "I believe," not "What I see." We are not to ask after or *observe* the "reality" in front of us. Does this mean, then, that Barth's "real" man cannot be observed? Surely, Barth's unreal man can be observed! Or does it mean that the one who does not realize the "reality" of man, in fellowship with God and his neighbor, is not yet human?

Hans Urs von Balthasar gently takes Barth to task on this

matter. On the one hand, he points out in Barth, human nature cannot be deduced from christology: rather, nature is left to its own research and knowledge. But on the other hand no scope is afforded to this knowledge. It is cut short by a reference to Christ as the true man, as though all other humanity were simply an epiphenomenon of Christ. Although Barth affirms that "the thing itself" is present in the copy, grace for him is not sufficiently bodily and natural.[39]

Barth does not do full justice to nature, to present reality and practice. Instead, nature and destiny, the definition and destination of man, the empirical world (man on earth) and the Word of God (man under heaven), are quickly jumbled, one overcoming the other. The penultimate and the ultimate, idea and reality, are "confounded," as Marx said of the idealism of Hegel. Earthly reality as the battlefield of God's kingdom is not to be found. There is not much of a struggle going on.

Connected with this concept of reality is another central feature in Barth's theology that leads him to describe sin as "nothingness" and the fall of Genesis 3 as an episode that is not of ultimate seriousness. This means that there is no real doctrine of sin in his *Dogmatics*. Sin is what God passed by and did not choose. Evil reality is not, then, a theme for theology. Barth's doctrines of man and salvation are basically conceived of in *supralapsarian* terms, apart from the fall. Thus we hear magnificent things all along—but they are strictly statements of faith, and to no extent of experience: A mighty airplane, very high up in the sky, but with no engagement of the enemy.

Unreality and intellectualism

If true reality lies in the other world, revelation must signify the disclosure of a reality we did not previously *know*. Wingren's chief criticism of Barth is that he participates in the modern change of the axle of biblical and Reformation theology. The question of man's *justification* has been re-placed by the question of man's *knowledge* of God. In the Bible and the Reformation the main issue was righteousness for the guilty and freedom for the imprisoned. In Barth, however, the dominant question is whether we have knowl-edge of God or whether there is in us no such knowledge, so that we must receive it from outside. This shift in the central question means that faith, which originally was the recep-tion of a new being, a new standing before God, a new obedience, and an alteration of the whole man, is now no more than a different knowledge, a new insight regarding God, an alteration in the thinking of man. Wingren points out that original sin now consists in wrong thinking and that faith becomes correct thinking; the verb "to think" actually dominates Barth's presentation.[40] Naturally this fits in well with the objectivism of the concept of faith in Barth, but it again leads his theology close to the idea of the "new self-understanding" that we find in Bultmann.

Wingren takes issue sharply with this intellectualism and its accompanying abstractions. He counters these as symp-toms of the unreality of God's work in Barth's theology. To show how inadequate such a view is, Wingren compares what God does for man to sending someone a check for one hundred dollars. The one who receives it certainly acquires the knowledge that it has been sent. But if he thinks this knowledge is the main point, and thus never cashes the check, he has a wrong view of three realities: (1) his own prior situation, as though lack of this knowledge were the decisive thing; (2) the real nature and function of the check; and (3) the nature of the sender. Wingren concludes that through Barth's work our attention in this generation has been diverted from the active and living God of the Bible who creates and who lavishes gifts upon us.[41]

A point to be noted in this regard is the striking sim-ilarity, as indicated before, between the theology of Barth and the system of Hegel, who like Barth had a pathetic concept of "reality" which had nothing to do with the real world and ignored evil. We recall the famous retort of Hegel, when a student commented that what he said bore little relation to reality: "So much the worse for reality!" Marx, however, wanted to put Hegel right side up again. He wanted to return from theory to practice and reality. Now that the realm of thought had been set up in Hegel's system, he insisted on moving into the realm of practice like "Themistocles . . . persuaded the Athenians . . . to found a new Athens at sea, in another element."[42] Perhaps Barth too will find his Feuerbach and his Marx. Bishop Robinson has already played something of the role of Feuerbach by transposing the objective contents of theology into the immanent I-Thou relation. And it may be that the attempt has already been initiated to put theory back on its feet again, to move on to human and social practice in the face of a harmonious theory and of man's discordant and alienated existence.

A Marxist test

The abstractionism of especially the early Barth was most keenly perceived—and welcomed—by the Marxist Milan Machovec. Machovec finds in Barth's theology a very sophisticated attempt to make possible the survival of religion in an age of atheism. This is so, he thinks, because Barth recognizes the atheism of practical secular life, (while) preserving the wholly other, the non-secular as a concern of theology. Machovec is not surprised that in view of the social situation in the twentieth century with its predominantly dechristianized way of life the main theoretical concern of Barth should be an attempt to exalt the central religious concept—the concept of God—so that it cannot be affected by secular conflicts. After severe defeats in all human affairs (throughout the eighteenth and nineteenth centuries) God must be kept out of everything secular if he is still to be defended at all in some way.[43] If speaking of God *in terms of* the world (*analogia entis*) has been progressively corroded by secularism, then before complete disaster strikes the opposing way of escape must be taken—through a "negative theology" that posits total discontinuity between God and the world.

The secularity of the world and secular development are no less presupposed in Barth than in the preceding liberal theology (for which the only way out was to level down the concept of God). In inverse form, according to a reviewer of Machovec's book, dialectical theology is also a child of its age: "Hence dialectical theology, as a theology of the twentieth century, in an age when science and secular life have already achieved absolute priority, proclaims the absolute transcendence of God and absolute discontinuity between the world and God. . . . Because men have become godless, and as a result of the socialist revolution will increasingly do so, these theologians tell us that there is no way from man to God."[44] In the long run, according to Machovec, dialectical theology simply confirms the truth of the Marxist criticism of religion: all theology is a mystification of a crisis in social development. "The 'real core' of the principle of the infinite qualitative distinction between God and the world, radical dualism, is to be understood as a mystification of the truth of atheism."[45]

Machovec thinks that Barth's insistence on God's transcendence, essentially a surrender of the secular world, which theological criteria will no longer help to shape, is a step forward. The more Christians enter into the humanistic engagement with practical life, the more the transcendent world of God—which, it is said, has nothing to do with this world—will fade into the background and finally disappear altogether as having no existential or social significance. Hence Machovec regards Barth as a stage on the way from Christianity to atheistic humanism. This way, he suggests, leads from Kutter and Barth to Hromadka and Bonhoeffer. He finally discovers in Bonhoeffer's *Diaries* an extraordinarily honest declaration of the bankruptcy of the religious *a priori* and a sincere desire to render service even under the presuppositions of an areligious age. Thus, for him, Bonhoeffer is the one who begins honorably to wind up theological history. Machovec sees in him "the logical conclusion of the two thousand year history of theology, of the science of God which has had to give up one position after another until it finally resolves to let go of its corner-stone, God himself."[46]

Machovec's conception of Bonhoeffer's quest for a "religion-less Christianity" may be grossly inappropriate (although not a few liberal theologians seem to tend to a similar view). Machovec, however, as an independent reader who is not committed to the interests of this or that theological school of opinion, buttresses our impression of the unreality of God at least in Karl Barth's early work, a stance which clearly can work into the hands of secularism, as far as concerns practical life.

BARTH'S LATER SELF-CRITICISM

Critical standards

Is Barth's theology, then, merely an understandable neurosis? Is it "a foxhole" in the no-man's land of fantasy? Something theologians invented to cope with reality? This is the question asked of modern theology by secular critic William W. Bartley in *The Retreat to Commitment*.[47] Heinz Zahrnt has the same concern regarding Barth: Barth "has shown theology the way to the Bible, but he has not with the same intensity shown the way back from the Bible to life."[48] How has Barth served the church? — or has he simply built a secret stronghold of transcendence,[49] a temporary refuge? Barth himself used to tell how a friend referred to the big volumes of the *Church Dogmatics* as the white elephants (the bindings are white in the Swiss edition). Some of his students replied that they were elephants indeed in size, and strong legs were needed if they were to stand solidly on the ground. The concrete history which precedes all dogmatics must be the front legs and the practical outworking of salvation must be the back legs.

Barth's own theological inheritance carried within itself the right standards for correction. From their teachers, Barth and his friends learned something essential about the concreteness of God's action. Johann Christoph Blumhardt, as Barth himself pointed out, had a passion for the reality and concreteness of the sin-forgiving power of the imminent kingdom of God.[50] Karl Barth's one-time teacher, too, Hermann Kutter, had stressed what could be seen in Blumhardt's life: that God's work in the world has its seat in concrete life and will necessarily relativize all mere theology. Barth himself put it well when he said that Blumhardt saw both the greatness of human need and the greatness of the divine promise. He saw them so intensely and viewed them so realistically that he expected the real, not just the intellectual, removal of the antithesis. His concern was to keep the real life of man in view and to bring the holy into this everyday reality, rather than relegating it to a holy place. Thus Blumhardt could not stop at an abstract objectivism of faith. He was constantly seeking the reality and the realization of what he believed. Barth had a clear grasp of the this-worldliness of God's work that impelled Blumhardt when he concluded that Blumhardt did not understand how people could say that the Holy Spirit is present if they did not also say where: He could not accept the idea that the words of the Lord are mere phrases and expressions, not to be taken as reality.[51]

Is not this the standard that theology must always hold before itself?

Barth's own teacher, Hermann Kutter (whom Machovec trims down to keep his argument smooth), presented the young dialectical theologians with the same critical caveat at the very outset. Although Kutter is very much the father of the stark objectivism of dialectical theology, he, who had once expressed his passion for both God and the masses in the formula "God—is the social question," soon began to dissociate himself from that objectivism. He told Barth and his friends that they had too much theory and too little concern for the multitude, the sheep without a shepherd. He coined a statement which is decisive for the criticism of all theology: "To actually *proclaim* God to a society that has fallen away from him is quite another thing than to differentiate a correct concept of God from an incorrect concept of God."[52]

The powerful tendency to transcendentalize faith also came under the criticism of exegetes, who were not so dominated by the various philosophical presuppositions of modern theology that they could not see what the text was actually saying. Thus Ernst Käsemann, writing about the center of the gospel—our Lord's teaching on the kingdom of God—issued a summons back from theological abstraction to the reality of concrete life. "It must be asked," he wrote in 1959, "whether Christ is the Lord of the world otherwise than in, with, and under his body, whether his world dominion can in any way be abstracted from the ministry of members of his body. . . . Barth is in danger of speaking of a *regnum Christi* which is abstract from the concrete ministry of believers and the reality of the body of Christ as the instrument of the *regnum Christi*. This opens the doors to metaphysics and mythology."[53]

Barth liked to insist that God is on his throne and that he conducts all things well, but what does this mean apart from people who obey his rule? Is the kingdom of God an exclusively other-worldly event that takes place even though we do not notice it and it does not change us? Not at all! It is realized in those people who enter it and follow the summons of the kingdom. For God's salvation is not just a sentence passed on the world as a whole. It takes concrete shape in the coming of the message through the feet and lips of missionaries. And it has a human side; it must be heard and received: "As therefore you received Christ Jesus the Lord" (Col. 2:6).

Barth himself saw and said this best at the very beginning and at the end of his published theological work. Thus, surprisingly, it is in Barth's own writings we find some of the few—and some of the best—statements in the whole theology of the twentieth century about the concrete reality of God's work. In these he makes clear that when he insists we cannot control God's work he is not implying its non-objectivity. He also brings out the distinction very well between what is non-observable and what *is* observable. In 1920, addressing a student conference at Aarau on the theme of "Biblical Questions, Insights and Prospects," Barth said that he personally was first influenced by Paul: "This man sees and hears something for which there is no comparison . . . which I do not see and hear for myself. But when . . . I wonder if I am having hallucinations, a glance at the secular history of the time, at the ripples which spread out in the pond of history, shows me that in fact a stone of unusual weight must have fallen somewhere into the depths, that among all the hundreds of wandering Near Eastern preachers and miracle workers who might have followed the same Appian way to imperial Rome, this one man Paul with what he saw and heard . . . must have set the most important things in motion."[54]

Here, *prior* to the emergence of dialectical theology, Barth found a more suitable metaphor for the subject matter of theology than the later one, now famous, of the bird in flight which can never be grasped or drawn with exactitude. To be sure, the Spirit is like the wind which "blows where it wills, and you hear the sound of it, but do not know whence it comes or whither it goes" (John 3:8). In this sense God's Spirit is indeed like the bird in flight, and an attempt at statistical description, though necessary from the human standpoint, is out of date even before it is complete.

But the subject matter of theology also includes the *work* of God, the *effects* of the Spirit, the circles that spread out in the pond of history. As Barth rightly observed, even if a person did not witness the "stone" going in, a "glance at the secular history of the time" indicates that *such big effects must have had a cause.* Barth's earlier metaphor also shows his keen awareness that God's work in the world is done through people who have seen and heard something of Him.

Barth's self-criticism

In his later years Barth actually turned a critical eye on himself and returned to this reality-related theology. The return began fundamentally when he made the theme of theology neither God alone nor man alone, but the disputed and offensive *center* of God's dealings with the Christian and the Christian's dealings with God. This is the point of his famous little book, *The Humanity of God.*[55] Also, in a later volume of *Church Dogmatics,* the world of man becomes again the locus of the Christian life: The Christian, as one who is called by God, neither should nor can flee from time and history in order to live essentially and really in another world beyond time and space. He lives in his time and history among other men. He lives wholly in this world. Thus, we are no longer induced to retreat to a metaphysical "fox hole in the no-man's land of fantasy" where no one can follow him, where he is unmolested — but also inactive. The Christian is now back on the disputed territory at the very point where Bultmann thought that modern man would gain the victory in the conflict between his own objectifying thought and the objectifying thought of biblical faith.

"The Vocation of Man," written during the final years of Barth's university work, is one of the finest sections in *Church Dogmatics.* In this section, Barth criticized his own earlier contribution to the theology of the unreality and pure transcendence of God, thus confirming our own observations up to this point. In the sub-section "The Event of Vocation," he first describes how the onesidedness of dialectical theology arose. It was a reaction against the subjectivism of the modern theology of Schleiermacher, Kierkegaard, and their disciples, for whom the human act of faith had become the central point in theology. We needed to learn afresh, Barth writes, that the Holy Spirit is the Lord and Master of faith and is not just identical with it. "Yet we also need to remember firmly again," Barth continued,

that the necessary reaction should not be carried so far that the historical and supra-historical presupposition is abstracted from this as its consequence, and therefore made in isolation the object and theme of theology. . . . This means . . . that the vocation of man should not be divested of its concrete historicity nor transcendentalized. We do not speak of it correctly, nor of God as its acting subject, if we speak of it docetically, as though it became and were real, true and certain only beyond the historical existence of man in time, as the work of God which is not also His work on man . . . as though the star which guided the wise men to Bethlehem finally shone upon an empty manger. In opposition to the previous error, we must not present the being and work and Word and Spirit of God as hypostasis which, even if with great majesty and glory, simply hovers over the mind and heart and life of man like a radiant ball of glass or soap-bubble, but never leads to the result that something happens. . . . In the vocation of man we have to do with an event in man's temporal life which to faith, but to faith very really, may be known as such. This is something which must not be questioned in any circumstances or on even the best of pretexts: not even for the sake of . . . an infinitely qualitative distinction between God and man . . . nor out of a rather tiresome concern lest the non-objective will be objectivized and the non-controllable brought under control if we take them with theological seriousness; and certainly not for fear lest we be thus betrayed into too great proximity to, or even into the very midst of, the Mystics, Pietists and friends of the community life both old and new. . . . We inevitably misunderstand the transcendence of God . . . and the *sola fide,* if we refuse to let B follow A, and therefore, cost what it may, to understand and describe the vocation of man as a genuine, concrete historical event in time.

It is, again, through what he finds in the Bible that Barth corrects himself:

It cannot be denied nor explained away that in all the stories of vocation in the Bible, from that of Abraham to that of Paul, while we certainly have to do with works of God or of Jesus Christ towards these men . . . yet because rather than in spite of this we are also dealing in the full sense with elements in their own individual histories and therefore in the history of the more near or distant world around them. . . . Upon them, and therefore at once upon the world around them, there came something which had in their lives . . . consequences . . . by which their further course was incisively determined, and in the power of which, wittingly or unwittingly, they exercised an incisive influence on the life of the world around. . . . The call of God makes heroes like Gideon, watchmen like Samuel, kings like David, prophets like Isaiah, Amos, Jeremiah and others, apostles like Paul, seers like John of Patmos—and all with the most far-reaching consequences.

Similarly, for those who came to know and could speak of vocation in the sphere of the Church, it was a work of God which came vertically from above, yet which was also just as real horizontally in their creaturely existence, so that it was an event which determined afresh their own time and that of the surrounding world. Calvin was right when he relentlessly traced back access to Christ to God's eternal election. But for this very reason he took it seriously as his own vocation . . .

and gave it prominence in definite acts not only in Geneva but in half of Europe during the sixteenth century. Again, John Wesley could give not only the date but the very hour of his own conversion, yet rightly he understood what happened in terms of the Lutheran doctrine of justification and therefore forensically and in terms of predestination. This did not mean, however, that he was forbidden but rather required to reorientate his life completely . . . and to enter a new way on which he had so revolutionary an external influence that without any exaggeration it has been possible to write a book entitled *England Before and After Wesley*.[57]

Thus far, Barth. In Volume IV of the *Church Dogmatics* the decisive character and the concrete form of man's sin are again grasped fully, and so also the effects of God's call to salvation are again understood concretely. Barth's statements contain as localizations all the relevant terms: space and time, noticeability, and history as the site of a divine salvation history working through humans—a salvation history through the existence of which the whole of human society lives. The examples from history speak plainly. Barth mentions by name individuals through whom the situation and the world around were changed. The "vertically from above" gives rise to horizontal and perceptible effects, as in Barth's earlier illustration of the rings in a pond caused by throwing a stone into it. For once, the sustaining element in the story of mankind is perceived in academic theology.

Barth has come right back. No longer does he try to shield theology from criticism by its full-scale transcendentalization. His theological aircraft is not bothered now by the enemy radar, or the arguments of secularism. He lets the effectiveness of God's truth in relation to the presuppositions of the modern world be God's concern. His theology now relates to the real dealings of God with man and no longer gives undue prominence to the boundary between this world and the world beyond.[58]

The corrective: Scripture

We have already pointed out that at the decisive point it was by looking at Holy Scripture that Barth was led to correct his theological statements. That this is the general center and motivation of Karl Barth's theology is stated by Eduard Thurneysen in his preface to the exchange of letters between him and Barth: Their great concern, and in the last resort the only one, was that the fountain of the Bible should flow afresh in our age.[59]

This is indeed the decisive corrective for all theology. Some statements that Barth makes about "The Upholding of the Community" when it is under the threat of secularization apply equally well to the upholding of theology.

> How, then, is it upheld? In reply to this question our safest place is to begin with the simple fact that right up to our own days the Old and New Testament Scriptures have never been reduced to a mere letter in Christian circles, but have continually become a living voice and word, and have had and exercised power as such. To be sure, they have sometimes been almost completely silenced in a thicket of added traditions, or proclaimed only in liturgical sing-song, or overlaid by bold speculation . . . or torn asunder into a thousand shreds (each more unimportant than the other) by unimaginative historico-critical omniscience. But they have always been the same Scripture . . . which can speak and make itself heard. . . . But at some point, as a fellowship of those who hear Scripture's voice, the threatened community begins to group and consolidate and constitute itself afresh around the Bible, and in so doing it again finds itself on solid ground when everything seems to totter.[60]

These statements describe fairly well the change that took place in Barth's own theology. Hence we may be very grateful to Barth for his later utterances. He is indeed to be "loved and honored" for having finally overthrown the idol of "non-observability" set up by himself and others. Not often in our own or other theological generations have we been taught the reality of God's work as clearly as by him. On the other hand, few in this or any previous generation have brought as much abstraction and other-worldliness into the church as the early Barth did for the sake of the objectivity of salvation. Unfortunately, this influenced a whole generation of pastors. As we have seen, Bultmann himself at one point felt he must criticize this early Barth from the standpoint of Scripture and reality. We are grateful indeed for Barth's new insight. It is correct. But perhaps Barth did not fully grasp the seriousness of what took place. In face of the crib and the cross, the earlier teaching represented by Barth and propagated by his followers—a teaching that for decades denigrated the quest for the historical objectivity of salvation—is not just "rather tiresome."

A theology of the unreality of God in relation to the world, whether it comes from Bultmann or Barth, distorts the essential element in Christian revelation and, in the long run, corrupts both church and theology.

4

THE COLLAPSE OF THE DOCTRINE OF GOD:

The Vanished God of Atheistic Theology

THE UNREALITY OF GOD AND ATHEISM: THEOLOGICAL ECLIPSE

WHAT AMOUNTED TO A deterioration and a dismantling of the Christian doctrine of God in a previous generation, turns into a complete collapse at the hands of a new set of theological spokespersons. Together Barth and Bultmann dominated theology for forty years. Barth's earlier theology and Bultmann's theological program describe the foundations of modern theological awareness. Where the schools join forces, they cast a shadow that has caused a complete theological eclipse. The transcendentalizing of God in the one way or the other has resulted in a devaluation of history. For Bultmann *what* happened is of no real account; and even the later Barth could still jest about theologians who "come out with swords and clubs" to lay hold of the historical Jesus.

Both schools castigated *experience* as a category that belongs to reality. Instead we find the demand for a pure faith not affected by the experience of altered reality. The Reformation principle—by faith alone (as distinct from *works*)—is changed into an antithesis between pure faith and the *experience* of faith. In this formula, experience takes the place of works, although it is as different from works as passive is from active. The total rejection of the experience of faith also tends to demand, contrary to the Reformation, a total rejection of the works that follow faith. There is a tendency, then, to overlook practice. As Wingren said with reference to Barth, the verb "to think" predominates, and intellectualism is installed in theology.

On the other side, Bultmann's central concept of "self-understanding" reduces Christian practice to intellectual activity.[1] Thus, the two most powerful theological programs of our time have regarded history, experience, and practice—in short, all the evidence of God's work—as almost theologically illegitimate. Consequently, they have very largely ignored them.

THE UNREALITY OF GOD IN THEOLOGY AT LARGE

The basic philosophical and theological theses common to Barth and Bultmann evoked great response from the very first. Barth himself has alluded to the numerous echoes of his initial teaching of the "wholly other" and the "infinite, qualitative distinction."[2] He was not thinking only of his own numerous students. The theology of the unreality of God's saving work formed a wide front with allied views still influential today, even in circles that do not honor Barth or Bultmann.

The "theology of the Word"

In the "theology of the Word of God," for example, Barthians, Bultmannians, and many others are united. This theology finds paradoxical expression in a phrase such as "The Word of God as Act." To be sure, God's Word is immediately also an act and it changes reality. The Hebrew language can thus speak of God's acts as his words. But the primary interest of the "theology of the Word" is not in God's deeds. On the contrary, a common mark of this whole movement is a lack of interest in history, almost to programmatic skepticism. Thus, a theologian of a very different stamp like Julius Schniewind, one of Bultmann's critics, nevertheless could say in a debate on the Lord's Supper that what happened on Maundy Thursday was not our concern.[3] This is perhaps why Schniewind and his group did not, and could not, speak a decisive word against Bultmann's program of deobjectification. The neglect of history in favor of proclamation, which was taken over from Kähler, is just another form of the same sickness. The pre-judgment manifest here led an Old Testament scholar, in protest against the unrestricted domination of "word-theology," to issue a necessary reminder to this whole school: Martin Noth argued that it seems to be not inessential, if we are to have an objective understanding of the Bible, concretely to examine the rootage of biblical history in the world history of the time, and not to bring against such an undertaking the charge of historical materialism.[4] In point of fact, in the past few decades we have reached a position, over a wide range of theology, that might be accused of historical immaterialism.

Unfortunately, the "theology of the Word" has largely dominated the field. Its remoteness from reality increased as it underwent a metamorphosis into a "theology of language," i.e. a theology for which God's work of salvation in the world became a "speech event." Perhaps there was perceived here, not without cause, another way of evading the demands of the "objectifying thinking of modernity." God's act as a mere "speech event" is the climax of the loss of reality in the "theology of the Word of God."[5]

Alibis for God

Still other forms of theology can compensate today for the unreality of God and his saving work. Thus, for example, the future as well as this-worldly or other-worldly transcendence can do duty for the reality of God. In some theologies today God's reality is exclusively future. Ernst Bloch, the philosophical expert on this view, judges it from the standpoint of consistently this-worldly Marxists: *Docta spes*[6] (the theological cousin of his "Principle of Hope") has the advantage over other theologies in that it has already broken with transcendence in the traditional sense. Others, of course, protest against a theology of the purely future reality of God: In a retreat from the present, it constantly postpones the point of realization, thus compromising its own seriousness. Thus a theology of the future may serve as a cover-up.

Worse, perhaps, than the theology of God's unreality in the present and the substitute of his reality in the future is the theology that finds God's reality only in the past. This is the religion of the scribes in every age. They are sure that God's reality and work will nowhere be found among us today, just as the scribes in Jesus' day were aware that God had been absent for a long time. But they are pious and know that God's work in the world was real once. They cling to this. They are essentially conservative. As the time to which they refer recedes more and more into the past, it often seems that they are destined to die out. They illustrate, however, something that we have already seen in the "theology of the Word of God": namely, that conservative forces, too, can vouch for the theology of the unreality of God. The front line in relation to God's absence does not run between right and left.

The unreality of God in academic theology

In the last four decades the influence of a theology of the unreality of God has been additionally enhanced by the dominant view of scholarship which has captured many theological faculties. For them theological scholarship often is a free activity of a small elite of scholars who may pursue their academic interest without regard for the urgent realities of practical life.

The abstractionism of this new ideal of learning has associated itself with the abstractionism of modern Protestant theology to give practical, academic expression to the unreality of God in the world. A dominant view of theology-as-science has long since forgotten Barth's demand that theology must be churchly science. Much of theology today seems to follow and adapt the motto of art for art's sake.

The material reduction of Christian faith to the act of intellection, thought, and understanding is confirmed by this academic outlook. Theology is no more than a set of theses which have no binding force and which change nothing. As Kierkegaard already observed, the medium for being a Christian has been moved from the world of ethics and existence to that of the intellect and metaphysics; Christianity has been reduced to aesthetics.[7]

Thus theology need never be more than theory. It lives in its own world. It is its own kingdom above reality, like a balloon detached from the ground. As Marx said about Hegel, dealing with this type of theory is not easy, for the demands of ethics and existence have all been anticipated. Everything is there—on the level of theory. Even the distinction between theory and practice is thereby blurred.

The separation of theology from life, society, and the life of the church is programmatic here. In academic theology there is little reference to reality, whether past or present.

This is an ancient fault of theology. It often treats history as the history of theologians, of men who may be known from their writings. According to this view the history of God's work in the world is a history of *books*. Paul says, however, that *people* are an epistle of Christ, not written with ink, but with the Spirit of the living God (2 Cor. 3:3). They are not documents of stone or paper, but living people who are witnesses to God's history with humanity. Speaking like that, Paul already shows that he was no regular university theologian.

One way to make God unreal is to historicize theology. This enables the theologian to avoid coming up against the question of present-day reality. The professor of church history can then say that he is simply a historian, and Old Testament scholars can seek their salvation in discussing how many spokes a Phoenician war-chariot had. We know many examples of this self-insulated movement of learning.

Thus some theologians have secretly turned into historians, philosphers, sociologists, and psychologists of religion. In face of the unreality of God there has been a headlong flight out of theology. The world-changing themes of Christianity have become no more than subjects of the history of literature.

When this happens the matter of theology is lost and theologians involuntarily confirm the old contention of atheistic criticism that theology has no subject of its own. It is high time that these idols of theoretical learning were overthrown, or in the long run we can hardly protest if another generation of theologians officially and openly change theology into an atheistic study of religion. Theology thus becomes the art of accomplishing its own abolition.

A maverick in German theology, Paul Schütz has called the abstractionism of academic theology the self-poisoning of Protestantism. He has no time for a theology which is a flight from existence and under whose tutelage everything in real life remains unchanged. Such theology demonstrates the disaster of the theoretical Christian—one can think this way, says Schütz, but cannot live it: The Christian faith ends in the intellectualism of the paradox. This kind of theology is simply theory *about* things; there is no access to the things themselves. But that means there is no Christianity at all. For Christ communicates only with the life that is lived. To be a Christian is not to respect the boundary, but to cross it.[9]

Schütz addressed these words to a young man in the

1930s. The problem has since grown to larger proportions. The refusal to put the question of the relevance of academic theological work to church and society has since become the subject of countless discussions. Simply working out the theory leads to withdrawal from real life. The Apostle Paul's declaration in 2 Cor. 3:3 can point to the fact that the loss of reality in theology ultimately issues in the loss of real people. We can lose people in pursuing research.

Some years ago a friend of mine, a theologian, had a remarkable dream in which he was led to a cemetery and to his own grave. On the stone he could not make out the date of his death but he could read his name and the terse epitaph: "He was too busy to care for people." In consequence my friend completely changed his allocation of time and style of life.

Academic theology today is like the young Justin Martyr when he was still a philosopher. At the end of a conversation on the shores of the Mediterranean an old Christian told him that he was obviously a lover of fine discourses but not a friend of deed or reality.[9] Justin took this to heart. Can theology do the same? So long as it remains an academic way of expressing the unreality of God it is preparing the way for transition first to practical and then to theoretical atheism in Christianity.

THE ATHEISM OF THEOLOGY AND THE THEOLOGY OF ATHEISM

The reaction against this domination by the theology of unreality was bound to come. J. Moltmann has excellently illustrated the surge of protest by a real incident. At the Ninth Conversation of Darmstadt, he reports, biologists raised the whole problem of the future of mankind. But theology, in the form of a lecture by a prominent Roman

Catholic theologian, looked above the concrete problems and sufferings of time to the "absolute future" which was God. This "very different, but real and essential future" was then interpreted as "the silent mystery of God." At this point the audience began to protest. One of them voiced the general impatience with this kind of theology when he cried out: "Here we have an example of the way Christians talk. . . . This theological prattle is without content or cogency, but it is put out as though it were profoundly significant, and it has something unusually intimidating about it. Its isolation from the concrete and imminent future which men are wrestling with here makes it completely irrelevant. . . . Such theological talk may be right but it is never to the point. . . . It could have been the same a thousand years ago and be the same in another thousand years. . . . One can evade the concrete tasks of today if one clings to the unaltered aspects of yesterday and even more effectively if one soars up to what is supposed to be the absolute." Moltmann concluded his report musing that theology and Christianity no longer know what they should be and what they wish to be. But the confusion of theology is no longer received as a profound and awe-inspiring paradox. We now hear of the "end of the closed season for theology."[10]

The "closed season" is ended for theology in theology itself as well, especially for the traditional theology of the unreality of God. Dorothee Sölle chose as a motto for her book: "Truth is concrete," and Hans-Eckehart Bahr attacked current trends in the theology of the Word of God on the pertinent ground that they reduce God's history in the world to an event in vocabulary.[11]

John A. T. Robinson was the first to throw out publicly the unused knick-knacks of a transcendental theology which had no obvious, or only very dubious, existential and social significance. According to the evident law by which one extreme always follows another in the history of theology, *a proclamation of the world without God followed the proclamation of God without the world.* Robinson's book initiated in church and theology a process that rapidly accelerated. The individual stages in this process are stations on the way by which theology is now pushing to a barely shrouded atheism.

Encouraged by parental instruction in the direction of an unconditional recognition of secularism, young theologians everywhere are now emancipating themselves from the heritage of the deobjectification of the gospel. Whereas their predecessors maintained the paradox of faith in God's existence on the one hand and his hiddenness on the other, they are now dissolving the paradox. They are stating positively what was earlier a blank. They are making a virtue of the necessity. The unreality or absence of God is explained by the fact that he is dead. Dorothee Sölle stated this in a metaphor common to this school: The gardener who cannot be seen or touched and who does not interact is just as good as no gardener at all.[12] The answer to a hidden atheism in theology is the open theology of atheism.

This development, not surprisingly, has serious consequences. We can see its consequences especially in the doctrine of God.

Paul Tillich's transcending of theism

At the end of his book, *The Courage to Be* (1952), Paul Tillich was already calling for at least the "transcending of *theism*" if not for a definite theology of atheism.

What does he mean by this? Tillich describes theism in three respects. One theism is that of popular political rhetoric which invokes God in justification of our own plans and interests. Here God is the agent of our own advantage. "God with us" is a slogan on our buckles and standards. This theism must be transcended.

Another is the theism of the proofs of God. This robs man of subjectivity and makes him a mere object of that God.

Over against it atheism is justified as a reaction against those stifling consequences. This theism above all must be transcended.

Between these two, but also as part of the whole which must be demolished, Tillich rather oddly includes a third theism—that of the Judaeo-Christian tradition. He describes this in unmistakable terms. It is the theism built on the more personalistic passages in the Bible. It stresses the I-Thou relation. It also stresses the ethical and social character of God's kingdom, the personal nature of human faith and the divine forgiveness, the infinite distance between Creator and creature, and finally, the person-to-person character of prayer.[13]

This is astounding. Is all this and not just metaphysics and philosophical theology to be left behind with the transcending of theism? What Tillich has to say about abolishing this heritage of faith is singular too, for in comparison with the many arguments for transcending the other two forms, his reasoning is of Spartan leanness here. Atheism, he claims, is a desire or effort to avoid this type of encounter with God. Thus the problem is existential rather than theoretical. But *why* biblical theism must be transcended if it is existential and not merely theoretical is not made clear. The one tiny observation on which the abolition of biblical theism is based is that "it is one-sided."[14] But this contention itself stands in need of proof. For the abolition of Christian faith in God on the ground that it is "one-sided" would never occur to a Christian who has learned to know anything at all of the exclusiveness of Yahweh, the infinite distance between Creator and creature, the I-Thou relation to God, the personal nature of the divine forgiveness, and so forth.

In place of the God of Abraham, Isaac, and Jacob, Tillich recommends a non-personal "God above God," and a "courage to be" derived from knowing that we are accepted and encouraged even though there is no one to accept or encourage us. This he calls "absolute faith": that is, faith without any information about who or what is believed. A private talent seems to be needed to acquire a taste for this kind of religiosity. If I were not persuaded to become a believer by an object, a vis-á-vis of faith, this kind of being-mysticism would be the last thing I should regard as necessary or desirable for life in the technological age (we have already discussed this aspect in relation to Bultmann).

A student of Tillich, Helmut Dee, has nevertheless attempted to sketch an atheistic view of the forgiveness of sins. The experience of forgiveness, he suggests, is an affirmation of being existentially affirmed even though there is no one and nothing to make the initial affirmation. Hence even one for whom the picture of a personal God and his work has lost all cogency can still have and proclaim the experience of forgiveness.[15]

This proposal was sharply criticized by Helmut Gollwitzer, who argues that the forgiveness of sins cannot be correctly expressed in atheistic terms, "because there has never been and never will be an atheistic Christian confession, proclamation and prayer . . . which no longer speaks of the acts of God." It was not an essential part of the Christian faith to view God as a person but essential to proclaim him as one who acts personally. A forgiveness of sins without God's action was hardly more than a self-claim to forgiveness, which was shameless in view of the real crimes that take place among men.[16]

The idea of a secularized atheistic Christianity or Christian atheism is meanwhile loudly promoted by many theological writers and publications. Negatively and critically, this entails the removal of those theological statements in which God is presented as acting subject. It means the amputation (D. Sölle) of theism in the three senses of the term as described by Tillich. Nevertheless, its proponents claim that the substance of Christian proclamation is being preserved in this process.

This brings us close to the extreme and most logical form of the theology of the unreality of God: namely, its inversion, a "theology" of the reality of non-God. In the theology of the unreality of God we saw only a partial and factual atheism which was not ready to become a specific theoretical atheism; now we get an outspoken, honest, and clearly verbalized atheism. That is a new phenomenon. A butcher recommending vegetarian fare would be an oddity, says an astonished Malcolm Muggeridge, but now for the first time in the history of Christianity theologians with strongly atheistic inclinations are commonplace.

The American Paul Van Buren, for example, on the basis of linguistic analysis, rules out all statements about God as essentially non-verifiable. He thus reduces the Christian message to a human perspective whose rise is *somehow* bound up causally with Jesus of Nazareth. In other words, Jesus of Nazareth once gave this way of looking at life the necessary expression. The result of this reduction is that theology is abandoned but christology remains. Van Buren thinks we have here only another form of the reduction which has been going on for a long time in other cultural spheres. Thus astrology has become astronomy and alchemy has been reduced to chemistry. Theology must go through the same process if it is to be a serious form of contemporary thinking.[17]

Dorothee Sölle's atheistic Christ

A similar view is championed by the German Dorothee Sölle in many books, articles, and radio talks. In what follows we shall be examining her essay "Is There An Atheist Christianity?" (1969) because it puts together very succinctly all her thoughts on the theme of Christian atheism.[18]

Sölle begins by proposing a third position alongside the traditional ones of theism and atheism. She explains her goal by referring to a conversation between three women in

Jean Paul's poem *Titan*, each of whom represents one of three positions. The first espouses the hope of immortality and represents the Christian tradition, setting God and truth apart from the reality of human life. The second favors a plain, positivistic atheism which can give no answer to man's questions and yearnings. She finally comes to grief in life in the person of its proponent. The third, when asked what she will do if there is no immortality or hope beyond the earthly sphere, replies: "I would love." This, says Sölle, is the voice of Christian existence in a post-theistic age.

In the rest of the essay Sölle tries to show that this new position is that of Christ himself, and she distinguishes it from traditional Christian theism.

It is evident that she—like Tillich—has in view not merely popular theism or philosophico-metaphysical theism, but also biblical and Christian theism: that is, faith in the life, reality, work, acts, and lordship of God.

She first separates "the design of Christ"—simply living as he lived, or neighborly love—from the "pharisaic and legalist temptation" which is always present in the church and which consists in thinking that in addition certain things must be believed about God. That both faith and life are necessary—a view which seems to be suggested by an actual study of Old and New Testament Scripture—is dismissed in advance as banal and stupid. For D. Sölle is out to establish an antithesis between faith and life. This antithesis controls her whole exposition. Toward the end it becomes the antithesis of dogmatics and ethics. But even before that it does a good deal of damage. For she has declared it to be the antithesis between theism and the "design" or ethos of Christ.

At first the two are set apart: The ethos of Christ does not presuppose a theistic view, even though Jesus himself was a theist. But the invocation of God does not add anything to his program.[19] From the parable of the Good Samaritan Sölle argues that theism and atheism have no bearing on the crucial thing which must be done if we are to be neighbors to others; they have no bearing on Christ's "design." The priest and levite were theists, or so we may assume from their calling, whereas the Samaritan was a quasi-atheist. It is left to us to infer that theism may in fact stand in the way of neighborly love.

This leads Sölle to the second stage of the principle which runs through the essay: namely, that *theism is an actual hindrance* to the realization of the "design of Christ" or the actualization of neighborly love. She hammers this point into our heads. According to her, the history of the church proves that theism, the relation of man to God, is in practice a way of justifying existing evils, either by declaring that the present state is divinely willed or by merely transferring its redress to prayer. Prayer, the essential mode of expressing theism, actually serves to throw all the responsibility on God and to leave it to him to change the world, so that man can sit back with folded hands. Theism was but an excuse for the lack of love. While offering the consolation of the next world, it facilitated ignoring pressing problems.[20] In other words, theism is not far short of being the root of all evil in the world. Ultimately, to preach God is to bind the hands of men. Sölle, however, does show some indulgence toward theism in the past. Men were then weak in the struggle against natural forces. So long as man himself could not make the world a secure place, his emotional need of a God superior to natural forces was understandable.

But this need no longer applies today. The bitter conditions of the past have been mostly eliminated now, says Sölle. The childish impotence of the race which was the cause of theism has been overcome in many areas and potentially so in others. The man who preaches God today perpetuates ideologically the ancient state of weakness. He fills men's minds with a false sense of misery.[21] This borders on the criminal, since it paralyzes man's attempt to help himself.

When D. Sölle argues that the real basis of deficiencies in production caused men to look to gods for help,[22] it is easy to see that she is close to the Feuerbach-Marx criticism of religion—and not merely in phraseology. The arguments against religion, which are as old as the hills, are all produced again.

The only new thing is that the program of Jesus himself is ranged on the side of atheism. Twice D. Sölle claims that if Christ were to come back today, he would be an atheist. For he would rely only on his world-transforming love. Theism, she argues, destroys his program by tying it to God and refusing love. "Authentic" Christian conduct today is in practice a-theistic conduct. Christ, we are told, did not pray to God. He helped himself. Christians must now do the same. There is no heavenly gardener: The garden is our affair. The climax, which is logical enough, is that Christianity stands in direct antithesis to faith in God. "Theistic conduct expects God's intervention, and this is anti-Christian."[23] Atheistic Christianity! We expect at any moment to be told that the second verse of the *Internationale* is the authentic Christian hymn: There is no higher being that will save us. We alone can overcome.

Having posed the alternative and instructed the Christian world, D. Sölle can finally state that the development of theology today is already going in the direction indicated by her. Admittedly, the former Secretary General of the World Council of Churches, Visser t'Hooft, could still say at Uppsala in 1968 that not giving help to our needy neighbors in the developing countries was *just as much* a heresy as rejecting one or another of the articles of Christian truth. But most of the younger theologians had already pressed on beyond this "just as much as." For them the vertical axis of faith, the relation between God and man, was subsidiary and irrelevant.[24] They were obviously following the path which Machovec already recommended: i.e. the way that leads from Christianity to Marxism. It is here that abandonment of faith in God has its main effect. As a sop to the older generations Sölle says in closing that while faith in God has no future one may still say (as did Herbert Braun) that God is happening, or eventuating himself, whenever neighborly love happens. In short, the familiar statement that God is love, which has always needed careful exegesis, is now at last summarily and authoritatively reversed: "The commandment and reality of love is God. There is no other reality of God than this one of ours."[25]

1. AN ALIENATION OF FATHER AND SON IN THE GOSPEL?

What are we to say to these new tidings? The program of Christian atheism obviously stands or falls with its separation of God and Christ. Atheism here is an "amputation" of the Father God from Jesus Christ. The true question which Sölle must put to herself and her followers is not only, then, whether Christian faith can survive this amputation, but whether the picture we have of Christ, and indeed the "design," life, and teaching of Jesus of Nazareth, can survive this amputation.

When D. Sölle says that God does not fit into Christ's program, she is suggesting that Jesus is only accidentally a theist, just as many people today say that of course they believe in God. But she is also assuring us that, in fact, Jesus acted without a "working hypothesis of God."

It is impossible, however, to describe the life of Jesus without taking his relation to God into account. Christ's dealings with the Father cannot be eliminated from his life. D. Sölle proves this herself when she has to take from Jesus his "childlike confidence in the Father" (which at least the New Testament speaks of) in order to make him religiously poor and hence to bring him into solidarity with the modern doubter. But this does not work out exegetically. D. Sölle's amputation of the Father is far more destructive than early twentieth-century doubt as to the "Messianic consciousness" of Jesus. Exegesis tells us that the address "Father" is one of the distinctive elements in the "design" of

Jesus. Even a cursory glance at the texts shows us that Jesus' relation to God (his "theism") is not an indifferent or accidental matter. It is intensive, personal, intimate, and all-pervasive. Jesus' dealings with God as his Father are an excellent expression of his love for God. He clearly loved God with all his heart and soul and strength, and his neighbor as himself (and even more than himself). To separate Jesus from his relation to God, or, more accurately, from his love for God, as though this were something contingent and nonessential is a gross blunder in view of what we find in the texts themselves.

It is characteristic of all the presentations of "Christian atheism" and the "death of God" that they begin with the laudable intention of offering a new translation of the message of Christianity in our day but end by offering only so many *free inventions* based on accidental fragments of the Christian tradition.

Perhaps this is why D. Sölle obviously distinguishes between the "design of *Christ*" and the theism of "Jesus of Nazareth," and goes on to speak only of the former. Perhaps she understands by "the design of Christ" something very different from the life and teaching of Jesus of Nazareth. If the program of Christ is detached from the person of Jesus, one can of course go ahead without impediment according to the principle that I myself will define what is Christian.

But what, then, is left of one's historical conscience and intellectual honesty? We do not dispute that someone may adopt this program for good reasons. But one cannot also say that this is an "authentic" account of the life and teaching of Jesus Christ, that it is genuine, tested, proved, based on the sources—assured and obviously appropriate, to use a few of Sölle's own synonyms for her favorite word, "authentic." Otherwise every possibility of meaningful communication is undermined. In short, we may praise the fact that "Christian atheists" still find a place for Jesus, or rather "Christ." But we wish that they would stick a little more closely to what we are actually told about him.

2. THE SEPARATION OF THEISM AND NEIGHBORLY LOVE

If Jesus made one thing clear, it is that the truth does not lie in sundering love of neighbor and love of God (D. Sölle herself has to make this separation even while bringing *the same charge* against theists in every age—another parallel to Feuerbach). This division is untenable. From the standpoint of the history of religion, it is absurd to claim that theism makes good deeds toward neighbors impossible. Why should faith in God and confidence in him always have to mean that we sit back with our hands in our laps? Already the Old Testament covenant at Sinai proves the very opposite. It shows that faith and action, theism and love of neighbor, stand in organic sequence. The same is true right up to the Epistles of John. Only a long period of disregard of the texts could make it possible to deny this. Christians may well have committed all the sins that D. Sölle and others allege against them both now and in every age, but they were never required to do so by the Word of God. The unconditional command of neighborly love has been enthroned precisely in the sphere of Judaeo-biblical theism and not in Herodotus, Epicurus, or Lucretius.

As we have shown repeatedly, the transcending of theism and the proclamation of Christian atheism are not just a new attack on the proofs of God or on metaphysics. What D. Sölle wants primarily is practical atheism: i.e. atheistic action. For her, as for Paul Tillich, the central theme is finally the self-determination of man. The real question is again that of the lordship of God. It is true that Sölle herself declares only cosmological and emotional theism to be superfluous. But she deals so constantly with voluntative atheism that she leads us to believe that in the first instance practical atheism, the atheism of will and deed, is the true gospel or program of Christ.

Perhaps D. Sölle mistakes Christ for Prometheus. The latter did not wait for the gods but helped himself. He, too, had a "love of man." But it is in him, if in anyone, that we find the assertion of an essentially unbroken atheism. To link atheism with the proclamation of Jesus makes "Christian atheism" an insecure, difficult, contingent, arbitrary, and ambivalent product. It is always to be feared that its proponents will finally decide that the linkage to the biblical Jesus is too bothersome and shed it, so that when the time of reckoning comes there will be nothing in the till. We do not hope this, but many precedents suggest it.

The end of theology

As for the question of God, the final description of love as God—obviously the hypostatization of human action—gives us no reason for confidence. The true content of Sölle's program, apart from the proclamation of neighborly love, is "authentic" atheism.

In "Christian atheism," the unreality of God in the doctrine of God has run its full course. The presupposition that God is dead is final. Theology in any clear and simple sense of the term is at an end. The hunt is over; the buck is dead. Voluntary and conscious atheism in theology, the so-called theology of atheism, is the *necessary inversion* of a purely theoretical theology in which it is only *believed* that God's Spirit is at work, but there is nothing in concrete experience or practice to correspond to or to vindicate the statement of faith.

The theology of atheism is the answer to the atheism of theology. The unhealthy theology of the unreality of God has now come to its death-throes. God is not dead, but this theology is dying. This is why theology is being replaced by anthropology and Christianity by humanism for the sake of further intellectual advance.

EXCURSUS: WHAT IS NEW IN THE NEW THEOLOGY?

Though modern programs claim to be new, they are not. Thus slogans like "the new theology" and "the new morality" actually held sway in theological journalism, e.g. during the period 1909-1910. R. J. Campbell was then the herald of a "new theology." In his book *The New Theology* he claimed that many dogmas—the biblical basis of divine revelation, propitiation, redemption, the punishment of sin, heaven and hell—are both erroneous and immoral. They run contrary to the scientific method which must be normative for our understanding even in matters of the Christian religion. This is why religion is now detached from life, he said. We preach to deaf ears because we no longer have good news. We cannot explain the problems of life. The main reason for declension from the church, which is to be remedied, is the fact that Christian truth is tied to expositions which thinking men have to reject completely on intellectual and even moral grounds.[26]

All this sounds very much like the propositions put forth by Bultmann and his pupils.

Paul Wernle, himself a liberal, reviewed the book. What was unacceptable, he concluded, was a theology of dualism and transcendence. In contrast truth brought a theology of immanence which rested on science and which was at the same time a theology of the kingdom of God as the theology of a victoriously advancing social movement. However, Wernle criticized Campbell's program as rather superficial in comparison with the heritage of the Reformation.[27]

In 1909, another commentator offered an account of the new theology which might well have been written quite recently. He stated that the twofold modern principle of all science and philosophy—immanence and evolution—was at the heart of the debate. There are those, he observed, who are convinced that the world will experience in the field of religion something similar to what it has experienced in that of natural science. The Ptolemaic view of the world would give place to the Copernican. In their view, as no educated person could now believe the older view that the sun goes round the earth, so the time was not far distant when all educated people will have abandoned the "older beliefs" in the religious field. It was also believed that the nature and beneficial influence of Christianity would be as little changed by this as the nature and effects of the sun were changed by the better Copernican understanding.

But this commentator was critical: The new theology had replaced the biblical gospel with an artificially-produced gospel which at important points stood in contrast to the traditional faith. What method had been used to get back to the source? Standards applying to ordinary reality had been applied to things that are beyond purely human experience and observation. Thus the scientific principle of the uniformity of events in time and space had been extended to cover the infinitely exalted and living God who is beyond time and space. Modern criticism thus eliminated in advance anything that was beyond the frontiers of natural knowledge, as though there were no longer any reality beyond those frontiers. This could also be said about Bultmann and his followers. In addition, we are immediately reminded of the generosity of the new theologians of our own time when Petri noted that confessions once defended with blood were now assigned to and granted value for their own age, but they were only husks without which we could not have the kernel, and now that they had done their work the time had come to scrap them—the argument that we can also hear today. Finally Petri noted that we do not have here a particular school or trend but a movement affecting the whole of Christianity which is aiming at no less than a reformation of Christianity in the sense of a new faith which will be plausible for natural thought.[28]

Petri was only one of many who fought the new phenomena. But were the phenomena so new after all? Not even then! Some observers of the movement at that time had the historical sense to see that they were not. Thus Paul Wernle argued that this theology had dominated intellectuals a century earlier; now it was back.[29] Others pointed out that

the principle that God is the immanent and not the transcendent cause of things is found already in the ethics of
Spinoza. In the ecstatic affirmation of being as such, of
which he heard so much in his day and which we now have
heard from Tillich, they found an echo of Nietzsche.[30]
Indeed, did not Nietzsche also already say that "God is
dead?"

Nevertheless, neither in the "new theology" of 1910 nor at
any other time did anyone claiming to speak for Christianity come even close to the contemporary allegation that
Christ himself was practically an atheist. More free religious
fancy is needed for this than an older generation possessed.
It takes a leap into irrationality which the older liberals
were far from making. One thinks of Ludwig Feuerbach,
now revered again, with his principle that God is dead but
we have to have some—humanist—religion. But this provides no answer to the astonished question which Frederick Engels put to Feuerbach: If God is dead, why don't
we turn to other matters?

Implications outside dogmatics

Hand in hand with the slogan of the death of God comes an
enthusiastic espousal of the secularity of secularism, an
ecstatic extolling of the worldliness of the world, and a
fervent "supersecularization of the secular" (as Norwegian
bishop Per Lønning put it at Uppsala in 1968) which, now
that God is dead and has been accorded a state funeral, can
be adopted as the object and theme of Christianity by
irreligious Christian man.[31]

The decisive criterion will henceforth be not the gospel
but the fact that the world is escaping us. When the will of
God need no longer be consulted, the question of the needs
of the time is all the more urgent. "The world sets the
agenda." Theology thus puts itself into a position where
from the start it is committed to chasing the tail of the

world. The ensuing after-the-event theologies document
their own lack of freedom. Submission to control by the
ideologies of the day, given out as progressiveness, is perhaps the reason for the many oddities in church and
theology today.

D. Sölle had already indicated how theology is to move on
from dogmatics to ethics. At the collapse of the doctrine of
God, the non-dogmatic implications of the theology of
God's unreality unfold before us. They may be summarized
as follows.

First, the "new morality" in Christendom is a direct
consequence of the lack of content in Bultmann's ethics and is
motivated expressly by his demythologization program.
The "new morality" is atheism, or the unreality of God,
applied to ethics.

Second, the inconceivability of God's work or the freedom of God from the world as an element of Barth's
theology is now utilized to set aside the Christian acceptance of the unchangeable moral commandments of God:
i.e. the decalogue. In this way theology, when discussing
penal law reform, for example, can ignore the general moral
law that was enshrined in state law and the way is cleared for
a secular conception of law. The proposition of "other-
worldliness" in Bultmann and transcendentalism in the
early Barth combine to promote an emancipation from God
and his commandments in the sphere of public law.

Third, it is increasingly evident that as a result of the
theology of the unreality of God, teaching and life fall apart,
especially with regard to the theory and practice of social
conduct. Atheism in ethics is followed by atheism in Christian social teaching. In this regard Reinhold Niebuhr's
middle period and its renunciation of Christian social
ethics and espousal of Marxist sociology provides a prominent example.[32] The more recent "Theology of Revolution"
is another.

The unreality of God and the march toward Marxism

Dorothee Sölle found she could not arrest her intellectual development with the ambiguities of the theory of "Christian atheism." More recently, she declared: God is not dead, God is—red! Christians must therefore be radical socialists.

This program of thought can be seen as paradigmatic for the path many younger theologians have taken. During the first stage, there was still satisfaction with theological theory. But then they were confronted with the reality of life, e.g. in industry or in social work, areas in which the place, point, and relevance of Christianity were hard to see. What difference did it make if a person became a Christian? Why should one become a Christian? The defects of theology became palpable here.

The question of reality was posed. A theological student once told me that he had studied the theories and concepts of Christianity for three years. He now wanted to know the related realities. More concepts, names, and languages would be no help. Is anything going on? Does anything change? This was the question. A "speech event" offered no satisfaction.

Theology and reality fell apart in the life of these younger theologians. Many followed the politics of Barth, but not his theology. They could no longer see the theological basis of their involvement. Their theology stood in no organic relation to their action. Having practice without theory, they were the best candidates for other ideologies.

Barth had hailed Feuerbach's criticism of religion as one of the few happy achievements of the nineteenth century. For it could be used against religious psychologists and other advocates of "religion" at the beginning of the present century. As for his own theology, Barth felt that God is so sovereign and exalted that Feuerbach's attack could not touch him—God was not a concept or idea. We have to see, however, what effect this transcendentalizing had on the younger generation of theologians. One man I knew was a member of a Communist study circle and a committed Marxist. As such, he underwent baptism and began to study theology. This phenomenon was new to me and I invited him to a debate. Throughout our discussion he referred to a long, dog-eared text book of Marxist philosophy. I asked him how the religious criticism, which is part and parcel of Marxism, could be reconciled with Christian faith. How could atheism and belief in God go hand in hand? His answer was that God is on high and is not touched by the Communist criticism of religion.[33] Perhaps so. But obviously this exalted God who is apart from the world also does not touch Marxist critics of religion, or Christians either.

If God does not determine the content and goal of action, he no longer determines the motivation either. Consistently atheistic friends of these young theologians do not bother to shoulder this basic contradiction in theory. They will soon point out to them that this remote God makes no difference in practice. Why, then, should they drag along a meaningless transcendence, the accidental ideological baggage of their personal past, when it has long since lost all significance for the daily struggle on earth?

I once asked another young theologian how he argued his social demands from his Christian faith, expecting a strong positive answer. But he told me with resignation that he had given up arguing theologically and now advanced only secular reasons. A profound loss of theory was thus brought to light. But the same applied to those at the opposite end of the scale too. Both political activism and political passivity—the two different attitudes in Christianity—displayed a complete lack of consistency regarding faith and action, between theological theory and real life. The link was already lacking at the level of theory or thought.

Not a few young theologians are taking this road today: If the world cannot be altered and shaped by Jesus Christ—we recall what Bultmann said about Christianity having nothing to do with shaping the world—then we must alter and shape the world without Christ: through Prometheus. This was the argument of the young Marx when he wrote that Prometheus is the "chief saint in the philosophical calendar." In the same way, many younger theologians, fed up with the theology of God's unreality, are now asking the question—and some of them have already answered it—whether they should not become Marxists in the full sense, including atheism.

Does not a sharp separation between God and the world—like Barth's earlier emphasis "God is in heaven and you are on earth"—lead ineluctably to this result?

Just one more instance. Early in 1968, I was debating the aims and content of my student work with some of my associates in the student fellowship. The point at issue was the thesis of one of the student leaders that "in an age of crisis" (in university politics, domestic politics, and the whole structure of society) *the question of God must be put on ice for a while.* I had actually heard that thesis in a number of places. What it meant was that for these young theologians, heaven and earth, God's action and the world's, had fallen apart. It was, however, decisive to realize that this view was the immediate product of the preceding years: with Bultmann's program it became logical and inevitable. This is what the students of theology had had to read. To turn to the world of work was to turn away from the question of God. But this temporary atheism would not be the end for many of them. When social problems do not cease to press—and how can they?—temporary atheism becomes permanent atheism.

What Barth said in 1923, when he spoke of "no objectivity, no upward grasping by man and no invasion of this world by the kingdom," and when he went on to speak of

Christians as those who, "not knowing about God and his kingdom, but knowing about the sighing of all creation, are united with what is honestly profane and not with the inanities of a theological contemplation of nature and history,"[34] he put the whole plight of *today's* theological situation in a nutshell. Barth unwittingly portrayed the course of theological development in the last few decades. This real atheism—the absence of God from the reality of man, nature, and history, the non-humanity of God (according to Barth's later correction)—demanded in reaction a comprehensive, positive secularism. The only difference between then and now is that the new generation is no longer satisfied with a mere "contemplation" of nature and history.

The discrepancy between society and the awareness of God is so much enhanced in modern Protestantism that an urgent need is felt to choose between the one and the other. People prefer to take up all kinds of irrelevant ecclesiastical or theological hobbies rather than to try to coordinate and integrate the question of God and the world of work, which will mean disrupting the peaceful separation of the world which has been learned heretofore, and hence taking a different view from that of honored teachers. Under a different banner, but with the same consequences, conservatives have waged the same fight against any "mixing of faith and society." The result is the isolation of the gospel. The great spiritual themes which once engaged and refashioned an earlier world now occasion boredom more often than passion. What traces do we find today of Barth's excitement when he marveled at "the great realities" that must have moved Paul?[35] In seminar lectures as well as innumerable Sunday sermons, we seldom get the impression that the solution to the riddle of history is at issue.

It is no wonder, then, that many people lose interest in the Christian faith. Why should they waste time on the religious poetry which is offered instead of the reality of God?

The modern theological alternatives—theoretical or practical atheism, temporary or permanent, partial or total, open or veiled—are all inadequate. Whoever is asked to choose between these different substitute-theologies should send the offer back. We need not put up with these mutilations of God's reality. God has given us a different choice.

THE REAL BASIS OF THEOLOGY: THE UNREALITY OF GOD IN THE LIFE OF THE MODERN CHURCH

There is in the church itself a parallel to this kind of theology. Millions within Christianity today are without concrete experience of the reality of God. They are disillusioned about God. In many places in the Western world, believers are on the defensive.

In the magazines and prayer letters of groups and movements of confessed believers one finds a good deal of life and a sense of God's presence. But one also gets the impression that the reality and presence of salvation often occur exclusively in the hours of fellowship on Sundays, at conferences and retreats. There is not much about an experience of the reality of God in vocational life. There is preciously little about solutions to personal or social problems in everyday life or healing of human brokenness and conflicts.

In this regard one has the sense that the typical stance is a defensive one. Does God really work only in our little Christian ghetto? If so, we represent a reflection of the incognito-of-God theology of the friends of secularism.

In Evangelical orthodoxy, one sometimes encounters a deep rift between theory and practice, which is the first sign of the factual unreality of God and a practical atheism. Here, a full system of faith and piety is still in place and is defended tooth and claw at every point. But here, as always in orthodoxy, it is often almost impossible to help the people concerned to an awareness of any other reality.

What's the problem? Everything has been thought of. But the point is that it has *only* been thought of. In real life, humanity faces the abyss.

Thus, at a student conference of evangelical persuasion which I attended I was proudly told that all the participants had a firm faith in God. But was there cooperation, discipline, and trust in God in the conference itself? Did people come closer to God and to one another? The leader had, in fact, to bear the technical and spiritual burden of the conference almost alone, and personal conversations showed that many of those present were in serious difficulties in their Christian life. They had enough to do to look after themselves. In theory everything had to fit in — but the reality was very different. Perhaps this is one of the reasons for the familiar reaction of many circles against Evangelical orthodoxy. The claim to stand at the heart of God's people is resented when no marks of this status can be seen. Believers should not take the criterion of reality lightly.

Evangelical orthodoxy (and, incidentally, each Christian group and congregation) has to face today the question of whether its practice is not like that of the scribal theology *which knows God and his work only in the past.* Is anything new happening among us? Is the old man being put off with his works? Is a new man emerging with new and good practices? Is anything changing? Or is the new thing which comes into the world with God's reality only a "new light" shed on the old circumstances, as in Bultmann? If so, Evangelicals cannot much criticize the Bultmannians.

Again, so long as they regard the Christian life only as an in-house affair, the best young people from their own ranks, who do not close their eyes to the discrepancy between theory and reality, will seek other goals for their lives.

Theology as an excuse for the lack of God

The same applies to the church at large. The tremendous concentration on church buildings and programs, which increasingly is simply using people and means to its own end—is not this perhaps a hidden atheism? The theologies of the non-objectivity and hiddenness of God's work can become the theoretical expression of the unreality of God in the church's life. What leads people to adopt this theology is not so much the pressing claim of the "modern self-under-standing" as a lack of experience of the reality of God's lordship. The theologies of God's unreality are an expression of what is acutally there—or not there—in church life. We have the theology we deserve. A lack of blood in Christian life produces an anaemic theology. Here is the deepest problem of western Christianity.

Recent writings indicate that the landslide in theological theory is caused by a lack of experience of God's working. One may recall what John A. T. Robinson said about prayer as soliloquy. That may be all there is, in the lives of many. Others point to the general drop in the standards of sexual ethics and the church's teaching on divorce. This must accommodate the experience of many pastors that there is no real new creation or healing of human relationships going on. The unreality of God in theology is preceded by a phase in Christian life in which theoretical theism is already accompanied by practical atheism.

The new reductions in theology could be accepted as reasonable theoretical steps, and establish themselves as such, only where and because they had long been accepted in practice by the division of God and real life into separate compartments and by the disappearance of the mighty works of God (Acts 2:11) from much of the church's life. Possibly some regular organizational church activity could then still, "in faith," be called God's working. This means that at the decisive point Bultmann was simply bringing to expression the secret of Protestant practice. Perhaps this is why his theology was so successful. It fitted the real situation.

The activity of the church under the unreality of God

The splitting of theory and practice itself takes a practical form today. If the spark of God's reality does not leap into the reality of the world, if we do not work with the gospel in the real life of man, two possibilities are open.

First, we may nurture a separate life of the church which can take shape and unfold at every level. Being a Christian will then mean participating in the church's life as in a complete, different world, having churchly interests, imparting and acquiring ecclesiastical knowledge, and perhaps developing a special form of churchly entertainment, humor, anecdotes, and a whole special folklore. Other satisfying forms of cover-up today are liturgical reform and enthusiastic experimentation in the reform of church structures. In face of the almost complete schizophrenia of the Christian consciousness and the almost unparalleled dissolution of theology as the nerve center of Christianity there is in this ingrown zeal something not unlike the feeding of sacred cows. The private and social irrelevance of this attitude is patent. Christianity then becomes an ethnic peculiarity among others.

This attitude can continue only so long as all is quiet in church and society. This is no longer the case. Pressured by the demand and inescapability of responsibility to the world we may then go to the opposite extreme and adopt a program of social action which for anybody reading church notices leaves the impression of a community college extension syllabus with everything from aerobics to travelogues. This second option, the appearance of which after so many years of a "theology of non-objectivity" can have the effect of a needed breath of fresh air in a stuffy and introverted church, in fact only confirms the existing dilemma. The way to the reality of the world is taken but all sense of the reality of God is left behind. Being a Christian and having a motivation to take up all these new activities are taken for granted; or it does not seem to have any bearing on the actual decisions. Practical application should be forthcoming, but it must be anchored in Christian commitment and confession if there is to be a movement from theology to practice.

If the two fall apart, the church fails to carry its message to the heart of humanity. It fails to help regenerate society at the core by applying the justifying and sanctifying center of faith. No "translation" is made.

The failure of preaching

This complaint applies above all else to the practice of proclamation in the church. Pastors have, in fact, proclaimed the separation of faith and life in countless sermons. The theology of God's unreality has found rich application here. For decades, God's reality has been detached from simple life and made so great and deep that no normal man can have any contact with it. We have made light of actual sins and taught men that the sin of remoteness from God alone was decisive. How this sin expresses itself in practice we have not asked. Hence, the justification, salvation, and sanctification of man become highly abstract subjects. Any life-setting is carefully expunged. There must be no simple, direct, practical, tangible, or naive understanding of faith. We have been made helpless. The only thing left for us to do was to absorb from the preacher the theological system he brought from seminary or constructed for himself. But what ordinary working person can do this? And of what use is a conceptual structure where the different steps represent nothing but distances in thought? The average layperson wants results and directions for his or her daily life.

Parents often find that religious instruction, too, shares the same dearth of reality. The materials are not down to earth; they bear no relation to daily life. What are we really aiming at, then, in preaching and Christian education? If we do not begin to bridge again the gulf between man and the message, the next step for the church's proclamation will be its assignment to the museum of ecclesiastical antiquities and the devising of a new and more relevant education which draws from other sources.

The splitting of the church

Until the change we are looking for finally comes, not merely doctrine or theology will break up into itself and its antithesis (perhaps we are still facing here the classical Protestant antithesis of faith and works?) but the church itself might also be split into two camps. The cleavage between personal faith and involvement in social reality can easily find organized expression in the founding of two parties. The one stands for orthodox confession and personal piety but does not believe anymore that all spheres of life, including the social sphere, must be molded according to the will of God. It draws apart and develops a theory that the shaping of the world has never been a concern of true faith. The other party accepts responsibility for the course of public affairs, but the meaningful relationship between its activity and the foundations of the faith is less and less evident. It is as though we were demonstrating today in the practical life of Christianity Barth's feeble dictum: "no grasping of man at that kingdom and no intervention of that kingdom in this world."

ATHEISM IN OURSELVES AND ITS CURE

What we must now realize is that the theologies that lock God out of the world—reflections of the actual state of the church—are an expression of our own quasi-natural atheism. In our own lives, even though we call ourselves Christians, the closed nature of the cosmic nexus and the autonomy of modern man are always present as a primarily ethico-existential reality. We are all infected with the practical atheism of God's unreality in church and theology.

This sickness has a long history in Christianity, as Jacques Maritain has shown: It is an endemic "itching of the ears" (2 Tim 4:3) which finds expression above all in the symptom of "chronolatry," the idolizing of the moment, of the spirit of the age, and of our own hearts.[36]

We should never ascribe guilt to theologians alone. Theologians, after all, have to do the speaking and writing, but when all is said and done, they simply reflect what a church actually knows and has of God's reality. Naturally, they increase and deepen our plight by stating it and if possible justifying it. But the root lies in us all.

What are we to do? "Wretched man that I am! Who will deliver me from this body of death? Thanks be to God through Jesus Christ our Lord!" (Rom. 7:24f.). The unreality of God in Christendom—this sickness can be cured. We do not have to accept the option of Christian atheism. We do not have to choose between a God without world and a world without God. There is a cure. Admittedly, as Maritain reminds us: a box on the ears cannot cure this disease of the ears. That would be poor medicine, for the trouble is due to malnutrition. It is caused by a deficiency of vitamins.[37] There is only one remedy against theories of the unreality of God: experience of the reality of God.

5

RECOVERING THE TRUTH:

Experiencing the Reality of God in the World

GOD'S WORK IN HISTORY

CAN HUMAN BEINGS FIND the reality of God? Can we have any experience of it? How are we to perceive God's reality and where are we to seek it?

The question at issue here is whether we must make the hiddenness of God our decisive presupposition as Bultmann does in his demythologization program and as Barth does in his earlier theology. Must we accept this hiddenness, view faith as nothing but a paradox, and say that there is no trace of the reality of God in the reality of the world? Or can we free ourselves from the tentacles of this theology of the progressive unreality of God? Can we work our way out of a theology that from the outset makes any perception of God's reality impossible, dismisses any expectation of such perception, and nullifies any attempt at it? If we cannot, Machovec's Marxist criticism is justified and theology topples into atheism. There is nowhere to stop along the movement from the hiddenness of God to the revelation of man.

Bultmann's doctrine that Christian faith does not carry

with it any distinctive events is unsatisfying. So is Barth's earlier thesis that God's reality touches the world only as a tangent does a circle, falling only on the crown of man's head. We must leave such theories behind.

It is not our present task to explore the question of the reality of God systematically. We are simply seeking orientation in the midst of the modern theological consciousness. Thus we want to give at least some considerations, observations, pointers, and indications that will help to free us from the drag of the theology of God's unreality.

The Perception of God's Work

God's work is manifest

In what follows I will try to show from the New Testatment what is hidden in God's work and what is manifest, what is invisible and what is visible.

Instructive for this purpose will be a survey of the use of the Greek stem *phaner-* (*phaneros, phaneroun*) in the New Testament. The word *phaneros* ("evident") first means "public" or "external," such as, e.g., the merely external nature of circumcision, which does not in itself say anything about the heart (Rom. 2:29). It is a surface change and hence may be "superficial." The opposite is "secret" (John 7:10). According to the conviction of the New Testament witnesses, there are some aspects of God's reality that are not yet revealed (1 John 3:2, Col. 3:4, 1 Cor. 3:13). But others are already manifest.

Manifest means that what is within takes outward form. The invisible is made visible in effects. Though the "flesh" (a human disposition) cannot be seen, the works of the flesh are manifest, and in them the disposition itself is also manifest (Gal. 5:19). Along the same lines there is also a *phanerosis* or manifestation of the Spirit of God (1 Cor. 12:7).

Both Spirit and flesh are invisible as the sources of behavior, but the respective forms of behavior are not. We have a good example of the use of the word *phaneros* and the conditions pertaining to the perceptibility of the reality of God in Philippians 1:13. Here Paul says that it has become manifest to the Praetorian guard that his chains find their explanation in Christ—that is, in his relationship to Christ. Notice first that the chains are visible. Second, the percept-ible fact of Paul's bonds is ambiguous; he may be in chains for some crime or political heresy. This ambiguity, however, must at least be in place. Only something visible—his hard, cold chains—can make his situation ambiguous in terms of its cause. If he were not imprisoned, there would be no ambiguity. There would be no question about the reason for his suffering and he could never contend that he was suffering for Christ. Third, because of its ambiguity, the fact needs to be interpreted and explained, and it is given its interpretation by what Paul says . Fourth, for those who are present in the situation Paul's explanation for the fact of his imprisonment is a good one. The evidence supports it. Paul's interpretation alone offers a full, consistent, and satisfying explanation of the visible fact. All other inter-pretations will, in the long run, entail contradictions.

Other passages in which *phaneros* occurs fill out the picture. To what degree Paul counts on a manifestation of God's reality in his works may be seen from 2 Cor. 4:10f., where he stresses the manifestation of the reality of God in the corporeality or bodily existence of the disciple of Christ: The life and death of Christ is worked out in the apostles, and indeed in their bodies. It can be *seen*.

Further, in contrast to Bultmann's understanding, the love of God which in itself is invisible, and remains so, is made manifest in an act or by action: "In this the love of God was made manifest among us, that God sent his only Son into the world" (1 John 4:9). In a similar fashion, the first letter of John also explains that love of brothers is a visible and perceptible sign of the invisible divine sonship of Christians ("doing righteousness"—a Hebraism that finely expresses the link between biblical faith and its ethical actualization). Both God and man make perceptible in their acts what is invisible in itself.

If the act of righteousness is visible, its invisible root and hence its correct interpretation may yet remain in doubt. But if there is no doing of righteousness, unquestionably there is something wrong with the life from the Christian standpoint. Another example is that Paul expects Timothy's growth in the faith to be "evident," visible to the eyes of the community (1 Tim. 4:15).

In his commentary on First Peter the great Evangelical exegete Adolf Schlatter commented, uninhibited by the contemporary theological disqualification of a term like experience: "The mark of God is his grace, which is not hindered or limited by anything. Its manifestation, which makes it an experience, is the call which grants a share in God's eternal glory."[1] In his discussion of Paul's phrase "manifestation of the Spirit" in 1 Cor. 12:7, Schlatter referred to the indispensability for human nature, that if a man who *thinks* and *wills* was also to *act*, the reality in which he is set should be perceptible.[2] The motivation for Christian action is directly related to the reality and perceptibility of salvation. If one of these is missing, the other will be too.

The "manifestation of the Spirit" serves the perceptibility of the divine reality. As Paul tells us, it consists in charismata, in God's gifts of grace to believers. Charismata, says Schlatter, are *"that by which the Spirit is made perceptible.* The word of wisdom and the word of knowledge are the most important endowment and the clearest *manifestation* of the Spirit."[3] Therefore, in the preceding verses the charismata are equated with, and explained by, the energemata or mighty workings of God's Spirit. In sum, Schlatter says: "The Spirit, who is in himself invisible, is made visible by his operations."[4]

That this is indeed the New Testament view has been shown by Wolfgang Schweitzer. With reference to Colossians 3:3, a favorite text of the theology of unreality, Schweitzer says that the hiddenness of our life with Christ in God is basically a very simple matter: The eternal life is hidden, but not the renewal of the way of life in this world.[5]

Thus, the reality of God is not to remain hidden but seeks to manifest itself. The saving work of God purposes to achieve, even in man, a perceptible practical alteration: that is, an alteration of his practice. For man's action is perceptible. Biblical statements about the emergence and qualities of the new man make this plain. Thus we are to put off the ways of the old man and do the *good works* for which the new man is created (Eph. 2:10).

Just as God's eternal power is to be seen in his works (Rom. 1:20), so the works of man bring to expression what is in him. They make the invisible "evident." This ability, the "production" of man (his conduct), is to be set in the service of the invisible reality of God which seeks visible effects in this world. Since the "passions and desires" — the motivating center of man — are changed and receive a new content, the external manifestation of the passions and desires, their "product," is also changed.

This basic anthropologico-ethical relation can be described by the phrase "fruits of being" (Jer. 32:19). Fruits are the acts in which the character finds expression. In their externality they are parallel to "works." Similarly, Jesus compares the relation of being and manifestation in men to that of a tree and its fruits. Good fruits are the goal, and for these we need a good tree. The fruits come last, and they can even be detached.

Both "works" and "fruits" are naturally visible and verifiable. However, observers who are outside can also get some idea where they come from. This, at least, is the view of Jesus, for he speaks of men "seeing your good works and praising your Father who is in heaven" (Matt. 5:16; c.f. 1 Peter 2:12).

How important this relation is, and how important is also
the objectivity, visibility, and perceptibility of the work of
God, may be seen finally from the reply Jesus gives to the
question of John the Baptist. He points to the works he is
doing, to the fruits of his activity, to what is being done
through him. He answers: Look, the predicates of the
messianic kingdom are here. Trace them back to their
subject yourself! *You* give the obvious, necessary, and correct answer.

This is the ongoing demand for faith, which cannot evade
the commitment to offer its own interpretation of the origin
and meaning of facts which it, too, at first finds ambivalent.
This is why Jesus must add: "Blessed is he, whosoever shall
not be offended in me" (Matt. 11:2ff.). There applies to
Jesus, too, what he said regarding others: "By their fruits
you will know them" (Matt. 7:20). So that is, after all,
possible.

Ambiguity and evidence

We have seen that God's work in the world is perceptible
even though we cannot prove that it is God's work. When
Barth says that the history of man is an endless ambiguity,[6]
we have to agree with him, for history is at all events
ambiguous.

But even this admitted ambiguity implies a certain objectivity and perceptibility of God's work in the world. There is
something, after all, that the eyes can see, the ears can hear,
the hands can touch (1 John 1:1), something that can be
perceived and known. What can be perceived is not, of
course, a conclusive demonstration. It has to be interpreted.
But it can bear the interpretation put upon it. The fact does
not not plainly contradict the interpretation. The interpretation is not without an object. The act of God and the act of
the Christian, the suffering of Christ and the suffering of
the Christian, are accompanied by an explanatory word

which sheds light on the act and suffering and makes them a challenge to those who see them.

Having established this, we now can accept what Bultmann said about Paul on the Damascus road in a qualified sense. Paul and others who came under God's working "did not experience anything special" in the sense that they did not experience, suffer, speak, or do "anything that is not human." Of course not. But this way of putting it sounds like the saying "Nothing human is strange to me." Is God's history with men only played out on the everyday human level? Does it merely confirm the human average, the all too human? Is there nothing more to it? The concept of the "human" is itself ambivalent. It includes the best in man and the worst in man, his greatness and his weakness. Do we have in mind the humanity of the priest and the levite of the Jericho road or the humanity of the Good Samaritan? The latter manifests the reality of God in history. We may thus say that the mere perception of events, acts, and experiences is accompanied by *greater evidence* for the theological interpretation, for the fact that God is at work and not the devil.

Demonstrability and perceptibility

The whole of the New Testament, then, assumes that God's invisible reality is made visible in the effects it produces in the reality of our human world and history.

Let us apply this finding to the presupposition of modern theology. If Bultmann said that justifying faith is not a phenomenon of existence,[7] he is right in the sense that God's justifying act, and even the act of motivation by which faith changes being, are not in fact perceptible. But the same applies to any motivation of human action. If it is said, however, that there *is* no alteration of existence by faith, and if Bultmann adds that justification by faith does not come to expression in existence, that the Spirit of God produces no mark upon a person's life, then we must demur. We were forced to assume that this is Bultmann's meaning by his conjoining of the immateriality of salvation with a purely forensic and declaratory doctrine of justification.

But surely Paul's experience on the Damascus road, which changed his life, can be verified by the consequences it had ("a stone of unusual weight must have fallen"). Did not this experience entail a break in his life, something new, a reevaluation of what preceded and what followed (Phil. 3)? Did not Paul begin to do different things after it, to speak different words, and to go different ways? Could Bultmann in the twentieth century even have taken up his pen to write his own statements if something momentous, and hence something verifiable, had not taken place at that time?

Obviously, we must distinguish between two words Bultmann seems to equate: namely, perceptibility (in the world) and provability.

We find the same difficulty in the early Barth. In his debate with Harnack in 1924, Barth allowed that God himself is human *reality* in the *person of Jesus Christ*. But for him it did not follow at all that this event can be also a subject of human, historical knowledge: if it is *this reality*, it cannot! The existence of a Jesus of Nazareth which may perhaps be known historically is not the reality Barth was concerned with. For Barth, there can be no direct historical knowledge of the historical reality of revelation.[9] As Bultmann immediately equated "visible" with "provable," so Barth equates "being *also* a subject of human, historical knowledge" with "*direct* historical knowability," rejecting both. But here we must differentiate: What is "directly knowable" comes, indeed, under the control of the human ability to know. But one may also conceive of a knowledge that man does not "know directly" or control in principle, but that is given to him.

We must concede that there cannot be a direct knowledge

of the reality of God. If there were, God's reality would be demonstrable beyond doubt and faith would not be needed as man's own commitment and decision. But it does not follow at all that the *results* and *effects* of God's action cannot be the subject of human, historical knowledge.

This distinction has been cogently presented by Otto Schmitz, a German Evangelical New Testament scholar.[10] "The non-demonstrability of the salvation event," Schmitz begins, "belongs . . . necessarily to its character as salvation event. If, however, the non-demonstrability of the salvation event is the only thing that can be said about its demonstrability, the danger arises that its character as salvation event will become a mere assertion which does not correspond to any effective reality in this world. The event . . . will then lose its credibility as salvation event."

Schmitz then gives two answers which, if we look closely, do not contradict one another. (1) "The salvation event of the New Testament cannot in any way be demonstrable for man": Thus, for example, the tension between Jesus' unconditional claim to lordship and the actual course of his history on earth is not resolved. Again, Jesus rejects the request for signs. The signs that do take place do not remove the unbelief of Israel. Access to the salvation event is not under man's control. It is hidden from "the wise and prudent." Nevertheless, (2) "this salvation event which is non-demonstrable for man is demonstrated to be the salvation event by the Spirit of God." Thus Jesus' unconditional claim to lordship is proved in the actual course of his history by the power of God. Mighty acts of God take place to aid faith. "The Evangelists often record that a divine miracle set those who experienced it before the reality of God's action" (Matt. 9:8; cf. Luke 5:20, Mark 2:12). The evaluation of signs as aids to faith corresponds to Jesus' own statement that his "works" lay upon us an even greater obligation of faith than do his words. The people were hardened in unbelief "*although* he had done so many works before them" (John 12:37). To the witness of the preacher is added, "as confirmation and as guarantee of its reliability" (E. Riggenbach), the witness of God through signs and wonders and powers and impartations of the Holy Spirit. "Paul too, in answer to the Galatians (3:5), appeals to charismatically effected deeds of power which have taken place among them and whose factuality there is no need to discuss." Furthermore the truth of Jesus is demonstrated by God's Spirit to the conscience of every man. This is shown in the controversies of Jesus, which never end in such a way that the matters at issue remain open and may be the subject of further discussion. The opponents of Jesus are convicted.

In sum, non-demonstrability and actual demonstration are not alternatives. Jesus sharply rejects the request for signs and wonders as a *condition* of faith, and yet he offers a plenitude of signs and wonders as an *aid* to faith. The distinction lies in the ungodliness and autonomy of man on the one side, which puts the request for signs as a condition of faith, and the praise of God on the other.

Demonstrability has man as its subject; man controls what is demonstrable. But demonstration has God as its subject; it thus confirms the freedom of God and the absence of human control.

The result in relation to our present question is that according to Otto Schmitz "we are not to doubt the divine demonstration of the salvation event because of its human non-demonstrability. We are not to make this event a mere assertion of faith to which there corresponds no reality of a specific work of God in this world. Its divine demonstration in spite of its human non-demonstrability protects it (i.e. the salvation event) both from the danger of a false objectifying and also from the danger of a false subjectifying."[11]

Those familiar with the Bible will probably find it absurd that I have taken so long to establish the fact that God's work in the world is real and that it is an object of human experience. This may seem obvious. But in the fact of the unreality of God in modern theology, there is an urgent need to maintain that, while God himself is certainly hidden, the traces of his work in the world are not.

Modern theology, on the basis of the text that "God is in heaven and thou art on earth," has radically separated God and the world. This was meant to be a new way of making man respect God. But, in the end, it has had the opposite effect. Even the Canaanite Rahab knew more and better things of God's true nature. Face to face with his mighty works, she sharply differentiated the God of Israel from her native gods: "the Lord *your* God is he who is God in heaven above *and* on earth beneath" (Joshua 2:11). In comparison, to confine God to heaven might easily seem to be the pompous expression of a pagan frivolity.

God's perceptible work is part of the exertion of his dominion. If we insist on the unknowability of his work, later—for good or ill—we shall have to insist on the unknowability of his will. But the people of God should "know therefore . . . and lay it to your heart, that the Lord is God in heaven above and on the earth beneath: there is no other. Therefore you shall keep his statutes and his commandments" (Deut. 4:39f.). God's work and God's command, God's saving activity and his saving ordinance, hold sway both in heaven and on earth until his will is fully done on earth as it is in heaven.

God's work in the world may be perceived; it is the content of human experience. We thus part company with the presupposition of the complete hiddenness of God and of his work in the world. This presupposition is an alien yoke, even if it is one that Christian theology has laid upon itself. The unreality of God and his acts, when advanced simply to "protect the uniformity of the modern world view," is a concession to the opinions of the day. It is a kind of voluntary idolatry. We must break with this. We must return to the "Augustinian presupposition that there is a work of the Holy Spirit that may be perceived in man and that Christianity is to be understood in the light of this verifiable divine operation."[14] We must proclaim the reality of God, or rather its *phanerosis*, its manifestation in works in the history of humanity.

THE WORK OF GOD IN HISTORY

For Old Testament faith and proclamation, it is certain that God reveals himself through historical events. Everything depends upon the work of God in history. This is especially clear when we realize that what seem to be nature miracles in the Old Testament are also related to salvation history. The sun stands still for the sake of Israel's guidance and protection. The cosmological and natural element is minimal, of secondary importance. Faith relates primarily to the sphere of historical reality and above all to the crimson thread of a history of salvation within secular history, of a historical canal which runs the whole length of the history of mankind.

The presuppositions of dialectical theology showed already that it did not stand in the same camp as the theology of the Bible. In the latter, the primary issue is not the cosmological difference between this world and the beyond, as in Barth's basic principle in *Romans*. The real problem is not in epistemology or ontology. It is in history and therefore in practice, in human action. The iron curtain or lid over the world is not in the first instance epistemological; it is ethical. Here lies the problem of man's urge and inability to achieve transcendence. For modern man the problem of the possibility of divine revelation is scientific and epistemological; for the Old and New Testaments, however, it is moral and religious.[13] All are included under sin and yet all should attain to righteousness. This is where the incapacity of man lies, and this is also where the work of God takes place: in the history of man's practical life.

We are not invited to forget this background when we turn to the New Testament. The Testaments are not linked merely by a common binding. It is plain at once in the New Testament that in the revelation of God in the life, death, and resurrection of Jesus of Nazareth, history is again the place and platform of revelation and revelation is history. It is beyond question that the New Testament witnesses themselves experienced, understood, and described the revelation of God in Jesus Christ as a sequence of real historical events. How could anyone who had been at the feeding of the five thousand say with the early Barth of the twenties that "our hands were and remain—obviously empty"?

The apostles perceived above all else the resurrection of Jesus Christ from the dead. Their preaching relates to a "divine, lifeworking creation which made itself perceptible in the fact that Jesus rose from the dead."[14] The resurrection of Jesus Christ from the dead is the key to the whole reality and perceptibility of salvation history.

Salvation history does not end with the New Testament. It stretches across the whole history of mankind as the history of the followers of Jesus Christ through and in whom he works. To it belong also the works which arise out of fellowship with him, done by his body. Jesus says of his disciples that they will do greater works than he does (John 14:12). They will demonstrate the workings of the Holy Spirit and declare to the people the name of the one who has worked them. God's work runs through the whole of human history in the change and renewal of people as this takes place in the context of the proclamation of the gospel of Jesus Christ and under the direction of the Holy Spirit.

Nothing new under the sun?

We have seen that the presupposition of the "modern self-understanding" supposedly carries with it the twin principle of the causality and analogical character of all historical events. Presumably under the dominion of this principle, Bultmann could not agree that anything new or special could take place in history or be done and experienced by humans. But this causal explanation of human actions and historical movements is unsatisfactory.

We have already objected to the way Bultmann lumps nature and history together under the rubric of causality. Bultmann's teacher, Wilhelm Herrmann, distinguished the reality with which the natural sciences deal from social realities. He thought it quite unacceptable to assume as real only that which is patient of scientific proof. He could even claim very generally that in history, which we can truly distinguish from nature, there is constantly taking place that which has never taken place anywhere before.[15]

The causality of history, which may resemble the causal nexus in nature, is especially broken in the history of human civilization. C. F. von Weizsäcker is astonished, for example, at the immense broadening of vision needed to even understand care for the old ones as a task.[16] Whence comes the conquest of biological egoism that we constantly find in history?

Do human renewals come out of thin air? This is already refuted by the fact that they are all obviously triggered by individuals. Can the workings of God's Spirit be understood purely in terms of natural causes? What caused the change in the life of Francis of Assisi and its broad historical consequences? What impelled Francis to kiss the lepers at the gates of his city and to care for them as the least of Jesus' brethren? Admitted, this is a human and not a superhuman action. But is it "nothing special"? In which sense? It is something which, theoretically, others and even all the others in that city could have done. But why did they not? Why did one begin to do it? A causal explanation would be more plausible if he had gone on living just as before.

But here (and everywhere in the story of the followers of Christ) causality is negated by the self-denial that characterized Francis' action. The model is the conduct and rule of

Jesus: "If any man would come after me, let him deny himself and take up his cross and follow me" (Mark 8:34). Where God's will is chosen and not human interest (see Matt. 16:22f), the natural course of history, the causality of materialism, the historical chain of human selfishness, is broken. There God's activity begins, and loving acts for people begin. The work of God is to be found in the history of the followers of Christ which runs through the history of mankind.

We could and should study here many other figures in the history of Christ's followers. For instance, what caused the seventeen-year-old Joan of Arc to aid France and to turn its defeats into victory? She herself said that it was God's direction. How are we to explain this upset in history brought about by an immature girl? What caused the English statesman, Lord Shaftesbury, to leave his family, social class, and style of life, to abandon this way of comfort, and in the event to become one of the first great social reformers for the hungry and thirsty masses of the modern age? Is this plausible? Is it natural, "nothing special," nothing visible? All these events are verifiable and they contain at least so much that is new and different from the common run that whole nations owe their existence to them.

Where God is present something new always happens that changes the world. New facts proceed from faith as faith itself is based on a new fact. Facts are, no doubt, ambivalent in their quality as signs and manifestations of the reality of God. Yet by their very presence they alter the face of the earth and make life possible for millions. "He who believes in me," said Jesus, "as the Scripture has said, 'Out of his heart shall flow rivers of living water'" (John 7:38). Men and women who are Christ's disciples are dispensers of life. This is true in terms of making life possible at all by material care, feeding children, contributing bread for the world. It is also true in terms of actually saving life, as Mother Theresa and her sisters do in Calcutta by taking the dying poor from the streets and ministering to them, healing rather than liquidating the people who are a problem. It is finally true at the highest level of care in terms of making true men and women out of people, "that we may present every man mature in Christ" (Col. 1:28).

The history of the work of God runs like a crimson thread through the history of mankind, sustaining and renewing it.

Oscar Cullmann has brought this out superbly in its broader context. The history of God's work, or salvation history, he says, is not a history alongside history. It is entangled in history and in this sense belongs to it. But it is not to be equated with it since it is only one thin line within history. Cullmann calls this the "progressive divine reduction." God chooses people and events through which he brings salvation to the world. The way leads from creation, by the whole race, then through Israel and its remnant to a single man, Jesus of Nazareth, and afterward it broadens out again to the apostles, the primitive church, the church of Jews and Gentiles and then the whole world. Mankind is the goal; the selection of a minority is the means to reach it. To neglect the first is to fall into non-biblical sectarianism. To neglect the second is to fall into equally non-biblical syncretism. The path of salvation history is universalism as end and concentration as means. God's work takes place, then, in the history of the race. A new form of the patristic teaching that Christ became man that man might be divine is, then, that Christ became history so that all history might be salvation history.[17]

God changes history

God works in history. In his works we see his reality. His reality comes into the world as a power of healing, transformation, and change. One perceives this in the person and work of Jesus. Jesus not only *is* something; he also *effects* something. In distinction from the scribal theologians around him he does not come only teaching what is good and healthy. Nor is he merely good in himself. Instead, he makes the good and healthy. The causative or creative characterizes him.

This is why the Bible speaks of the *power* of God and why Paul says that the preaching of the gospel is always accompanied by the "demonstration of the Spirit and of power." It testifies and demonstrates at the same time. It adduces the evidence of an altered reality so "that faith might not rest in the wisdom of men but in the power of God" (1 Cor. 2:4f.).

The power of God comes into the world with the Holy Spirit. The Spirit works as the one who transforms. The Spirit changes the world by changing men. *The Spirit leaps the barrier between the other world and this world.* Through the Spirit, through God's indwelling in man, the reality of God is at home on earth. The Spirit is the great Realizer; he realizes the counsels of God.

The lack of a controlling concept of the reality of God in modern theology corresponds, therefore, to the long-recognized lack of a strong doctrine of the Holy Spirit in Protestantism.

The Spirit works in the life of people. We remember that the later Barth, in his great self-criticism for the deobjectification of salvation history, mentioned specific names: Abraham, Moses, Gideon, Samuel, David, Isaiah, Paul and John, also Calvin and Wesley. The reality of God speaks concretely out of the lives of people. Common to all of them is the fact that they made space and time for the work of God in their lives.

Later in his life, Barth summed up excellently what needs to be said about the work of God and its manifestation in history:

> All time is potentially the time of grace, and all history the history of salvation. Indeed, we must say that they are the sphere in which, as the Lord of all men and the one to whom

they belong, Jesus Christ . . . is actually on the way . . . to His
victory. . . . His call is a creative call which rings out as a *Fiat*,
and as it does so there comes into being that which was not . . .
a new history . . . not merely internal but external, not merely
spiritual but moral, social and political, not merely invisible,
but also visible. And in the world around the man who is called
. . . even though it may not be noticed, this history will at least
call for notice, and . . . it will certainly not be without relevance
and significance for the history of this world around and for
human history generally. It will thus be a history which itself
makes history.[18]

It is interesting to see how the later Barth answers the
question of the perceptibility of salvation history. It "may
not be noticed" by those around but "it calls for notice." We
observe also how precisely he describes the way in which
the reality of God lets itself be known: "not merely spiritual
but moral" (what scorn Barth's theological generation had
heaped on this word *moral* which represented ugly objectivity in ethics!), and then "social," and finally "political
history." And indeed in this order. The work of God begins
by changing the thought, will, and action of individuals and
then goes on at once to have effects in their social environ-
ment. Too often theology has shown little interest in the
history of the followers of Christ and the realization of the
kingdom of God. The result has been to obscure the thread
of salvation history which links us today with the revelation
of God in Jesus Christ. Here, for once, academic theology
tells us what is the sustaining element in history and where
we may find the reality of God.

In conclusion, we emphasize therefore that Christianity
is not an idealistic philosophy, like Platonism, with cultic
elements added. The decisive difference lies in the history
that it is based on. This is the fundamental difference
between Greek thought and biblical faith. In order to
understand God, the Greeks speculate; the Israelites,
though, look at the events of their liberation from Egypt,

and the Christians at the life, death, and resurrection of Jesus of Nazareth. It is this difference which some theologians have failed to address.

Hope for Christianity

Missionaries tell about a remarkable phenomenon in northern Nigeria. On a cliff there, one may find the oversized print of a human foot and alongside it the no less large print of the foot of a dog. Natives call this the "trace of God." It is the task and the glory of theology to point to the traces of God in history and to help people find the right path. Traces of God are to be found everywhere in the history of the disciples of Christ. This history is not "obviously empty." George Müller, who founded the great Bristol orphanage, made it a rule never to solicit funds for the support and extension of his work except from God himself. But there constantly came to him the hundred dollars—to use Wingren's analogy—and much more. He and his charges would not have been helped by mere "information" and the "pure faith" which rejects any fulfillment of the promise lest it become impure. Müller's example also shows, however, that the lifegiving work of God is not under man's control, as theologians rightly emphasize. God's work is particular. It has the nature of a sign. It creates models of the new life. It is not in our grasp; we cannot bank on it—God is free. But we may pray and hope for his work of grace. We have the promise that "if you then, who are evil, know how to give good gifts to your children, how much more will the heavenly Father give the Holy Spirit to those who ask him!" (Luke 11:13).

Confronted, however, by the development and condition of present-day Christianity in the West, even in face of this promise, one might ask in doubt: "Son of man, can these bones live again?" (Ezek. 37:3). We know what answer Ezekiel was privileged to see. Jesus has also shown to us the great kindness of God our Father in his parable of the lord who forgave his servant an enormous debt "because you besought me" (Matt. 18:32).

Under the forgiveness of God we shall again learn to love God, and God will again cause good things to be done through us. This is why the old bishop in Alan Thornhill's play *Hide Out* says with confidence that sometimes when he sees the fiery windows of the cathedral he knows it is not too late. The fire can come back and purge the selfishness and shabbiness from our lives, beginning with the church.[19]

The church's chance lies in the faithfulness of God to penitents. Peter Howard put this well when he wrote to a friend of mine: "Do not be too discouraged if sometimes you fail. Few of us are saints. Certainly I am not one. My decision is to stay at the heart of the battle and carry Christ's cross with Him regardless of how anybody else behaves or misbehaves, or regardless of how I behave or misbehave myself. 'The blood of Jesus his Son cleanses us from all sin' (1 John 1:7). This is an everlasting truth, moment by moment, to all men who turn their eyes and hearts to Him."

NOTES

Chapter 1. DISMANTLING THE TRUTH: Bultmann's Program of Demythologization

1. Immanuel Kant, *Critique of Pure Reason*, III, III (London, 1884), pp. 359ff.

2. For the dominance of the concept of analogy in historical study, cf. E. Troeltsch: " . . . the means by which criticism becomes possible at all is the application of *analogy*. The analogy of that which happens before our eyes . . . is the key to criticism. The illusions, . . . the formation of myths, the deceptions, the party spirit, which we see before our eyes, are the means of recognizing such things also in tradition. Agreement with normal, usual, or at least variously attested, happenings . . . as we know them, is the mark of probability for happenings which the critic can recognize as really having happened or can leave aside. The observation of analogies between past events of the same kind makes it possible to ascribe the probability to them and to interpret the unknown aspects of the one on the basis of the known aspects of the other. The omnipotence thus attaching to analogy implies, however, the basic similarity of all historical events, which is not, of course, identity. . . . " Quoted in J. Moltmann, *Theology of Hope: On the Ground and the Implications of a Christian Eschatology* (London, 1967), p. 175.

3. Rudolf Bultmann, "Bultmann Replies to his Critics," in *Kerygma and Myth, A Theological Debate* (hereafter cited as *KM*), ed. H. W. Bartsch (New York: Harper & Row, 1961), pp. 191-211 (cf. p. 210).

4. R. Bultmann, "New Testament and Mythology," *KM*, 1-44, quoting from p. 6.

5. Ibid.

6. R. Bultmann, "Zum Problem der Entmythologisierung," in *Kerygma und Mythos*, hg. H. W. Bartsch, vol. II (Hamburg, 1952), p. 182 u. 2. (Not in the English translation which at this point is curiously truncated.) (Emphasis added.)

7. *KM*, p. 5.

8. *Kerygma und Mythos*, vol. II, p. 184 (not in English translation).

9. *KM*, p. 3.

10. *KM*, p. 9f.

11. *Kerygma und Mythos*, vol. II, p. 185 (not in English translation).

12. *KM*, p. 11.

13. *KM*, p. 33.

14. *KM*, p. 41.

15. *KM*, p. 117.

16. *KM*, p. 43f.

17. *KM*, p. 36.

18. *KM*, p. 44.

19. *KM*, p. 111.

20. *KM*, p. 117.

21. *KM*, p. 37.

22. *KM*, p. 66f.

23. On this point cf. also E. Bloch, *Atheiusmus im Christentum* [Atheism in Christianity] (Frankfurt, 1968), p. 32.

24. *KM*, p. 7.

25. Carl Friedrich von Weizsäcker, *Die Tragweite der Wissenschaft* [The Relevance of Science], vol. I (Stuttgart, 1964), p. 169 and cf. p. 170: "The infinity of the world is a symbol of naturalistic belief."

26. Karl Marx—Frederick Engels, *Collected Works*, vol. III (New York: International Publishers, 1975), p. 304f.

27. This observation suggests that one must examine whether atheism as a denial of God's existence and work is not primarily a denial of his lordship. Denial of God goes negatively through the same movement as does the confession of God in the Old and New Testaments. Both historically and qualitatively what comes first here is not attestation of God's abstract existence, but attestation of his lordship and of the implications of this claim in the historical life of man. Hence denial of this claim in relation to both world history and ourselves is a mark of atheism. We ourselves want to rule. Atheism is seldom an intellectual cosmological decision based on research and insight. It is usually an existential and historical decision which is made prior to observation of reality.

28. Von Weizsäcker, *op. cit.,* p. 171.
29. *KM,* p. 6.
30. *KM,* p. 30.
31. *Zeitschrift für evangelische Ethik,* 11 (1967), pp. 218- 230.
32. The Jewish philosopher Hans Jonas, a former pupil of Bultmann, has tried to correct Christian theologians at this point. In his address "Heidegger und die Theologie" (1964) he said that the theologian who is true to himself cannot make a system of historical destiny, reason, or eschatology the framework of his own teaching, whether it be that of Hegel, Comte, Marx, Spengler, or Heidegger. The reason why he cannot do this is that such systems belong to this world. Concerning the world the Christian has learned that it has its own law (whether reason or fate), its being, its power, its voice or voices ("the rulers of this world"). From such a system he can indeed learn *what he has got to deal with*: i.e. the nature of the principalities and powers, to whom he is subject as a creature and as a citizen of this world. But he cannot adopt their views as a basis for understanding his own message, which stands in radical transcendence of God whose voice does not come from being but breaks into the sphere of being from outside. Hence Jonas challenges his "theological and Christian friends: Do you not see what you have to reckon with?" (*Evangelische Theologie,* 24 (1964), p. 630.
33. *KM,* p. 11.
34. *KM,* p. 10.
35. It helps to clarify matters that Bultmann refers to the early work of his student Hans Jonas in this regard. Jonas in his book on *Augustin und das paulinische Freiheitsproblem* (1930) has an excursus on "The hermeneutical structure of dogma" (p. 66). In this he sets forth as the methodological basis of demythologizing the fact that some concrete experience underlies even the most remote and metaphysical hypostases. Arising from these experiences we find the basic motifs which lead to the hypostases of dogma. The latter then are hypostatizings of *something*: i.e. something originally and existentially demonstrable. While Jonas himself applies this thesis "in an exemplary fashion" to the Gnostic tradition, Bultmann sets out to demythologize the "mythology" of the New Testament along the same lines (KM, p. 16).
36. On this cf. E. M. Blaiklock, *Layman's Answer: An Examination of the New Theology* (London, 1966), who contrasts the terse language of the New Testament accounts with the Gospel of Peter (the gigantic size of the risen Christ) and the Protevangelium (the cosmic pause at Christ's birth).
37. H. Braun, "Gottes Existenz und meine Geschichtlichkeit im Neuen

Testament," *Zeit und Geschichte, Festschrift für Rudolf Bultmann*, ed. E. F. Dinkler und H. Thyen (Tübingen, 1964), p. 400.

38. *KM*, p. 34.

39. *Kerygma und Mythos*, vol. II, p. 184 (not in English translation), cp. *KM*, p. 10 n.2.

40. K. Frör, *Biblische Hermeneutik* (Munich, 1961), p. 41. Cf. also H. Ott, *Geschichte und Heilsgeschichte in der Theologie Rudolf Bultmanns* (Tübingen, 1955), p. 28.

41. Frör, *op. cit.*, p. 35.

42. Frör, *op. cit.*, p. 43. Cf. H. Gollwitzer, *The Existence of God as Confessed by Faith* (Philadelphia: Westminster Press 1965), p. 59, who speaks of the *elimination* of all objectivity and facticity.

43. *KM*, p. 21f.

44. R. Bultmann, *The Gospel of John: A Commentary* (Oxford, 1971), p. 617.

45. An odd fact is that Bultmann in his *Theology of the New Testament* (English translation New York: Scribner's Sons, 1951), can give many excellent expositions of biblical concepts. Cf. what he has to say about the Holy Spirit as both the miraculous power which is given to believers and also the norm of their conduct (p. 336). In the process of demythologizing, this two-fold function of the Spirit which conjoins theological and anthropological statements as indicative and imperative is reduced to the uniformity of anthropology, for now the theological aspect simply renders the meaning of the anthropological and historical data. But when the idea of power is cut out, Bultmann's own concept of the "act of God" is left hanging in the air. We cannot conceive of "power" apart from its concrete effects.

46. *KM*, p. 21f. (The analysis which follows here demands a more literal translation than the official English translation offers.)

47. An instructive and momentous uncertainty regarding the subject and predicate of theological statements is found by Gollwitzer (*The Existence of God*, p. 15) already in Bultmann's early (1925) essay: "What sense is there to speak of God?"

48. *KM*, p. 22.

49. We thus find the same sequence as in Jonas's methodological principle, in which basic human experience comes first. Cf. what Jonas said in 1964 about the demythologization program, and his own part in its development, in "Heidegger und die Theologie," *Evangelische Theologie*, 24 (1964), p. 641: "If Bultmann thinks that Heidegger's analysis of existence might give a better explanation of the Christian understanding of man than some mythological terms of the New Testament, it has to be added: yes, as far as man is concerned, but not as far as God is concerned. Even if analogies are

being made, the understanding of God cannot be a function of man's self-understanding, or you will end up in immanentism. Existential terms can stretch only so far as the sphere of their verification, i.e. phenomenology, goes. They can include man's experience of himself *before* God but not his being *in* and *from* God. In Pauline and Augustinian terms they can include man under the law but not under grace. Where in faith the divine itself enters into the inner dynamic, i.e. in the so-called demonstration of the spirit and of power, the love shed abroad in our hearts (Rom. 5:5), phenomenology is silent, and with it the verifiable concepts of existential knowledge, and with these demythologization too. And even more so when the mysteries of the Godhead itself hold the floor."

50. Cf. L. Feuerbach, *The Essence of Christianity* (New York: Harper Torch Books, 1957), pp. 19-21, 25, 60. For Marx, cf. "Notebooks on Epicurean Philosophy," in Marx—Engels, *Collected Works*, vol. I, p. 458, and in his "Economic and Philosophic Manuscripts of 1844," *Collected Works*, vol. III, p. 34.

   For a more detailed study of Feuerbach's method of criticism of religion which basically has become the Marxist method of criticism of religion, see my book *Leiblichkeit und Gesellschaft. Studien zur Religionskritik und Anthropologgie im Frühwerk von Ludwig Feuerbach und Karl Marx*, 2nd ed. (Giessen/Basel, 1980), pp. 69ff., 195ff.

51. *KM*, p. 13.

52. *KM*, p. 196.

53. *Kerygma und Mythos*, vol. I, p. 184 n.1 (not in English translation).

54. There are of course philosophers who dispute the antithesis which Bultmann posits here. They would agree with Christianity when it says that being is a gift. Bultmann rejects this as ontologically impossible: philosophers of this kind must be rudimentary Christians. *KM*, p. 30.

55. *KM*, p. 31.

56. *KM*, p. 32f.

57. *KM*, p. 33.

58. D. von Oppen, *Das personale Zeitalter* (Gütersloh, 1967), p. 133.

59. *KM*, p. 43.

60. *KM*, p. 23f.

61. J. B. Soucek in *Kerygma und Mythos*, vol. I, p. 151f.; G. Wingren, *Conflict in Theology* (Philadelphia: Muhlenberg, 1958), p. 142f.

62. F. Buri, "Entmythologisierung oder Entkerygmatisierung der Theologie," *Kerygma und Mythos*, vol. II, pp. 85-101.

63. It is a similar contradiction that we should still read the New Testament at all. The basic offense is that a specific persona is preached to others. The resurrection on the third day contains no

particular offense beyond this basic offense. On the other hand Barth in his *Rudolf Bultmann—An Attempt to Understand Him* praises the inconsistency: Bultmann should command our love and esteem for the fact that at one point at least (to the annoyance of F. Buri) he has broken away from existentialism; cf. *Kerygma and Myth*, vol. II (London, 1972), p. 116.

64. *Kerygma und Mythos*, vol. II, p. 97.
65. H. Gollwitzer, *op. cit.*, p. 57, argues in contrast that the presupposition of the particularity of an event which is bound to the name of Jesus is essential for Christian theology.
66. H. Braun, *Gesammelte Studien zum Neuen Testament und seiner Umwelt* (Tübingen, 1962), p. 294.
67. Ibid., p. 303.
68. "Zeit und Geschichte," *Festschrift für Rudolf Bultmann*, p. 415.
69. In evaluating Braun, Bultmann himself reaches the impersonal formulation that true faith is not acknowledgment of some image of God, however correct this may be; it is readiness for the fact that "the eternal" (*das Esige*) will ever meet us in the present; cf. *Glauben und Verstehen*, vol. IV, p. 126.
70. H. Braun, *Gesammelte Studien*, p. 341.
71. Ibid., p. 335; cf. p. 282 and *Zeit und Geschichte*, p. 407.
72. Ibid., p. 338.
73. Ibid., p. 431 (*"Gott ist das Woher . . . vom Mitmenschen her"*).
74. Ibid., p. 297.
75. Ibid., p. 431.
76. *Gesammelte Studien*, p. 272. One is reminded of the original methodological thesis of Jonas.
77. Ibid., p. 341.
78. *Zeit und Geschichte*, p. 408.
79. *Loc. cit.*
80. *Gesammelte Studien*, p. 298.
81. Ibid., p. 341.
82. Ibid., p. 297.
83. Cf. H. Gollwitzer's *The Existence of God as Confessed by Faith*. It is the merit of Gollwitzer that he opened the debate between Christian theology and modern theological atheism. His work is one of the best of our time, for it conducts its analysis against the background of the history of European thought and philosophy of which we get only sparing glimpses in the theology of the last two decades which is hand in glove with existentialism. Gollwitzer also deals with something that is for the most part sorely neglected in present-day theology: namely, the role of Marxist thought, the most vital ideology of secularism, as the horizon of these discussions.

84. H. Gollwitzer, *op. cit.,* p. 94f.

85. Ibid., p. 63.

86. It is worth noting that God is also the "whence" for Schleiermacher, *The Christian Faith,* §4,4; cf. Gollwitzer, *op. cit.,* p. 92 n.3. The glee with which Feuerbach greeted this type of theology should be remembered: "I am so little against Schleiermacher here that he serves in fact to confirm my own assertions" (*Sämtliche Werke,* vol. I, p. 249).

Chapter 2. THE SURRENDER OF REALITY: Repercussions of Bultmann's Approach

1. *KM,* pp. 191-211.

2. Ibid., p. 192.

3. Ibid., p. 192f. Bultmann largely disregards the danger that exposition of Scripture—the attempt to discover Scripture's own evaluations and judgments—might be subjected to the evaluations and judgments peculiar to "guiding concepts" (drawn from philosophy). He ignores the danger that exegesis might no longer be open to what is disclosed anew. Bultmann agrees that the exegetical work now becomes dependent on philosophy, but he feels that we can go ahead without anxiety, for the necessary methodological concepts are supposedly strictly formal or neutral and will not anticipate any material decisions. Furthermore, alteration of the object of investigation will be prevented by the "simple" fact that the philosophical work which is presupposed will be one that is concerned to develop in suitable concepts the understanding of existence that is given along with human existence itself. (*KM,* p. 192f.) The word "simple" is designed to impart confidence, but in fact it does the very opposite.

4. Frör (*op. cit.,* p. 40) has shown that the function of this concept is no longer questioned by Bultmann, not even when he says that as the expositor hears the word of the New Testament he must be ready to correct the ideas he has brought with him.

5. H. Ott (*op. cit.,* p. 28) points out that the application of Bultmann's concept of myth means as such that an important decision is made prior to all exegetical encounter or concern. This consists in a specific pre-understanding of reality.

6. *Kerygma und Mythos,* vol. II, p. 106.

7. Bultmann obviously feels that his category of self-understanding is the conceptual counterpart of the principle that we can know of God only what he does to us, which was developed by his teacher Wilhelm Herrmann. But this principle already reduces the field of

God's action in the same way. It is not biblical. We can also see what God does to others. Thus the Canaanites, prior to the Israelite invasion, can gain a view of Yahweh which commends respect by considering what he has already done for the Israelites. Cf. also the crafty Gibeonites in Joshua 9:9ff.

8. *KM*, p. 44. This self-understanding alone constitutes in the last resort a zone which is isolated from the closed and causally connected sphere of the cosmos, and can thus be rightly proclaimed as religious territory. (H. Thielicke, in *KM*, p. 152.)

9. The degree to which the concepts chosen by Bultmann involve selection, judgment, and a straitjacket for the tradition finds expression in Bultmann's well-known statement that he finds the stories of the exorcism exercised by J. Christoph Blumhardt "preposterous" (*KM*, p. 120). This is a typical value judgment. The stories shatter a separation between this world and the beyond, and so what ought not to be cannot be. The real question, however, is whether the events took place, not whether they please us.

10. *KM*, p. 117.

11. G. Wingren, *op. cit.*, p. 142.

12. *KM*, p. 43.

13. This is better expounded in Bultmann's *Theology of the New Testament*: "Only because man is *soma* (body) does he have the possibility of being good or evil and having a relation to God" (p. 198). Here we see how better exposition can arise without the control of a philosophical program. How can such a statement go over with the principle that the Christian faith means other-worldliness and must have nothing more to do with the objective world?

14. Cf. E. Schweizer in *TDNT*, vol. VII, p. 1063, where it is pointed out that Paul's scars show that he belongs to Christ already in the body. It is essential for Paul that his faith and discipleship are worked out in the whole of his bodily life and not just in a purely intellectual or emotional sphere. God's rule or the rule of evil are to be found in corporeality. A. Schlatter says that Christ wants our acts and members, not just our knowledge (cf. *Paulus, der Bote Jesu* [Stuttgart, 1956], p. 202); the corporeality of man is not "indifferent." Only the autonomy of the body and its desires is overcome and ended; cf. A. Schlatter, *Gottes Gerechtigkeit* (Stuttgart, 1952), p. 212f. on Rom. 6:12f. In the Old Testament, as in Jesus and Paul, we find no purely cosmological or scientific interest in man's body, just as there is no such interest in the world in general. It always goes hand in hand with an ethical interest. This is supposed by Schweizer's statement (*op. cit.*, p. 1065f.) that what interests Paul is not the looks, abilities, or character, but the acts of the body and what happens with it. In

this sense the objectivity of the body and the world is always of concern for Christians.

15. The world is the world of man, says, e.g., Karl Marx. Inversely he is expressing the same point when he calls nature the greater body of man without whose material changes man would not exist at all. (*Collected Works*, vol. III, 275f.)

16. H. Plessner, foreword to his pioneer work *Die Stufen des Organischen und der Mensch. Einleitung in die philosophische Anthropologie*, 1928, p. vf.

17. *Op. cit.*, p. 195f.

18. H. Ott, *Geschichte und Heilsgeschichte* . . . , pp. 181ff. on the individualistic element in Bultmann's thinking. This is the phenomenon that led H. Thielicke to turn Emanuel Hirsch's criticism of German idealism against Bultmann.

19. *KM*, p. 150f.

20. G. Wingren, *op. cit.*, pp. 147, 131.

21. *KM*, p. 203.

22. *KM*, p. 22.

23. H. Ott, *op. cit.*, p. 17 n.1. Cf. already A. Oepke in *Kerygma und Mythos*, vol. II, p. 171.

24. Ibid., p. 18, Ott quoting Bultmann's *Glauben und Verstehen*, vol. I, p. 61 n.1.

25. Ibid., p. 28.

26. Ibid., p. 34.

27. H. Ott, *op. cit.*, p. 26. In view of the relation between theology and ontology at this point we are reminded of the saying of Hans Urs von Balthasar that he who is blind to being is blind to God (*Rechenschaft* [1965], p. 31).

28. Ibid., p. 50.

29. Ibid., p. 37.

30. It is interesting to compare Bultmann's own objection against Barth many years earlier: "If faith is beyond consciousness, is it a real thing at all?" (*Anfänge der dialektischen Theologie*, ed. J. Moltmann, vol. 1 [Munich, 1962], p. 130). This question must now be raised again — against Bultmann.

31. Thus Bultmann argues that if the task of demythologizing was demanded by the conflict between the mythological view of the Bible and the modern scientific view, it was also true that demythologizing is a requirement of faith itself; *KM*, p. 210. What a happy coincidence, one is tempted to say, if one were not forced to consider what Barth said in *Die christliche Gemeinde in der Anfechtung* in 1942: In the history of the church there is a type of temptation which leads some people to maintain "that in the voice of

the age is to be heard a particular moving and whispering of the Holy Spirit. For them, therefore, there is no conflict. . . . They do not merely say that there has to be some outward yielding in certain circumstances. In the name and language of the gospel, with profound theological arguments, and not without appeal to the Bible . . . they claim that this or that change or renewal in life or teaching, which is accidentally the same as what others want to thrust on the community from without, is inward and right from the Christian standpoint; it is the command of the hour." K. Barth, *Theologische Fragen und Antworten, Gesammelte Vorträge,* vol. III (Zollikon-Zurich, 1957), p. 297. This whole essay is very much to the point.

32. *KM,* p. 39; "dangerous" for whom?
33. *KM,* p. 199.
34. *KM,* p. 199.
35. *KM,* p. 210.
36. *KM,* p. 200.
37. The same verb *synhistemi* occurs also in Rom. 3:5. According to T. Zahn, quoted in F. Rienecker, *Sprachlicher Schlüssel zum Neuen Testament* (1956), p. 321, it means "to establish something which is actually there but is not obvious immediately or to everybody."
38. *KM,* p. 121.
39. The ambivalence of a tangible phenomenon which has to be present as such if it is to be interpreted, has been dealt with by Hans Freiherr von Campenhausen in his study "Der Ablauf der Osterereignisse und das leere Gran," *Sitzungsberichte der Heidelberger Akademie der Wissenschaften, Philos.-histor. Klasse* (1952/4; 3rd ed. 1966). Von Campenhausen offers a convincing answer to the question of the resurrection and to the question of the relation between fact and meaning.
40. *KM,* p. 41f.
41. *KM,* p. 211.
42. *Loc. cit.*
43. *Loc. cit.* Bultmann's abstractionism is perhaps demanded by his idea of the closed nature of the objective world, but many figures in the history of Protestant theology can also be invoked. It is not for nothing that he employs a purely declarative, nominal doctrine of justification (without the new creation and the new birth which in the New Testament and the Reformers are the other side of the story) as the basic mode of his thinking. As in his view the non-observability of both sin and the new life is emphasized, there the justification of the sinner is viewed as only "theoretical," in God's judgment. The fact that God's judgment is also a creative word which

changes the reality of man is ignored. It is once again worth noting that in his *Theology of the New Testament*, Bultmann gives a far more accurate account of the Christian doctrine of salvation. The philosophical presupposition seems to control his more programmatic utterances.

44. *KM*, p. 199.

45. *KM*, p. 191f.

46. *KM*, pp. 24, 20.

47. Fritz Lieb, "Geschichte und Heilsgeschichte in der Theologie Rudolf Bultmanns [on Ott's book]," *Evangelische Theologie*, 15 (1955), pp. 507-522; references are to pp. 514, 516, 517f.

48. Ibid., p. 517.

49. K. Marx.—F. Engels, *Collected Works*, vol. III., p. 175.

50. *Collected Works*, vol. IV, p. 53. As Marx wrote, "A non- objective being is a non-being" (*Collected Works*, vol. III, p. 337).

51. *KM*, p. 211.

52. F. Buri in *Kerygma und Mythos*, vol. I, p. 100; F. Lieb, *op. cit.*, p. 516; H. Ott, *op. cit.*, p. 200.

53. *Glauben und Verstehen*, vol. II (Tübingen, 1956), p. 137f.

54. It is true that in a note Bultmann does consider the distinction between nature and history as two different spheres of reality, but he rejects it: "Historical study understands history as a self-enclosed whole" (*Kerygma und Mythos*, vol. II, p. 182 n.1). Admittedly, Bultmann continues, a non-materialistic science of history differentiates the course of history from that of nature, for it sees intellectual forces and personages at work in history so that there is no element of physical necessity in what takes place. Nevertheless, what takes place does so with a motivation that can be understood. Here, then, is the closure which makes the reality of history the same as that of nature. They are one reality over against the idea of a divine intervention.

55. Human action and history is the very field of religious or philosophical motivations: "Religious and ethical convictions relate to human action and can be demonstrated only by human action, whereas scientific convictions relate to facts" (C. F. von Weizsäcker, *Die Tragweite der Wissenschaft*, p. 112).

56. *KM*, p. 35f.

57. R. Bultmann has an appreciation of Smith's book in his essay "Der Gottesgedanke und der moderne Mensch" (1963), *Glauben und Verstehen*, vol. IV, pp. 113-127.

58. *The New Man: Christianity and Man's Coming of Age* (London, 1956), p. 49 (where this kind of transcendence is claimed as characteristic of the Old Testament), pp. 94ff.

59. Ibid., p. 111.
60. *Gesammelte Studien*, p. 334.
61. Ibid., p. 341.
62. "Exposition and encounter" is what happens to us in terms of word and fellow-man, *Zeit und Geschichte*, p. 410.
63. Both J. A. T. Robinson and R. Gregor Smith perceive this. Robinson accepts Feuerbach's inversion of theology to anthropology and has to confess that this brings us on to dangerous territory, for it might end up deifying man (*Honest to God* [London, 1963], pp. 49ff). Smith, on the other hand, hails Feuerbach's attack on the existence of God, and the innerworldly interpretation of theology. The only problem was that Feuerbach called his conclusion atheism, which was not at all necessary.
64. H. Ott, *op. cit.*, p. 200.
65. Cf. the impression made on Ernst Bloch: "a substitute which in its own way reminds us of a mere stopgap, inward this time, but at what a lowered and even shocking price. On what a slender branch that which has lost its high position comes creeping out, and for forward movement it has no courage and no world, especially no new world . . . "; *Atheismus im Christentum*, p. 18, and cf. especially p. 69: "It is the private straw of this self . . . of what is allegedly purely individualistic (divorced from the social and the secular), which remains to the rump Christian of this type. The bodily, social, and cosmic are all dismissed as secular, as world. The soul does not need to bother about them."
66. "Indifferentism (the term actually used by Bultmann) became itself the most tyrannical of theories. . . . The very conception of the Church as an independent moral authority, whose standards may be in sharp antithesis to social conventions, had been abandoned. An institution which possesses no philosophy of its own inevitably accepts that which happens to be fashionable. . . . The surrender had been made long before the battle began . . . a spiritual blindness which made possible the general acquiescence in the horrors of the early factory system. . . . The abdication of the Christian Churches from the departments of economic conduct and social theory" brought to light the underlying blindness: "It did not occur to them that character is social [and society spiritual]." R. H. Tawney, *Religion and the Rise of Capitalism* (London, 1948), pp. 192, 196, 271, 275.

Chapter 3. A DETERIORATION OF THE DOCTRINE OF GOD: Barth and the Unreality of God in the World

1. M. Machovec, *Marxismus und dialektische Theologie. Barth, Bonhoeffer und Hromadka in atheistisch-kommunistischer Sicht* (Zurich, 1965).

2. Kurt Frör, *op. cit.,* p. 35.
3. Bultmann acknowledges this commonality in his review of the second edition of Barth's *Romans;* cf. *Anfänge der dialektischen Theologie,* ed. J. Moltmann, vol. I (Munich, 1962), p. 121.
4. Cf. *Glauben und Verstehen,* vol. I, p. 146.
5. K. Barth, *The Epistle to the Romans* (London, 1933), pp. 314, 318.
6. K. Barth, *Christmas,* as quoted in G. Wingren, *op. cit.,* p. 26 n.6.
7. R. Bultmann, in *Anfänge,* p. 120.
8. Ibid., following Barth's *Romans.*
9. Ibid., p. 121, quoting from Barth's *Romans.*
10. Ibid., p. 130.
11. Ibid., p. 132.
12. *Romans,* p. 195. Note the parallelism in the deobjectification of the salvation event in Christ and in the Christian life today. Rudolf Bultmann stuck to this common point of departure: if Barth spoke of an event which does not take place among the other events, Bultmann writes in 1952 that the divine event is not one that interposes itself between secular events (*KM,* vol. II, p. 197).
13. This comes close to Bultmann's language of "self-understanding." Also, in both Barth and Bultmann the work of God is supposed to consist in the creation of "possibility," not the reality of the new life.
14. *Romans,* p. 221.
15. Ibid., p. 223.
16. "As though" is a frequent expression in the second edition of Barth's *Romans;* cf. pp. 141, 224, 314.
17. I. Rilliet, quoted in Hans Urs von Balthasar, *Karl Barth. Darstellung und Deutung seiner Theologie* (Cologne, 1951), p. 402.
18. Karl Barth, *Des Christen Wehr und Waffen* (Zollikon, 1940), pp. 5ff.
19. *Romans,* p. 318. No great step to Braun's statement that he resolutely remained within the limits of this world and that he regarded these limits as closed from the standpoint of the laws of nature and history.
20. Karl Barth, *Protestant Theology in the Nineteenth Century* (London, 1972), p. 641f.
21. K. Mittring, *Heilswirklichkeit bei Paulus, Neutestamentliche Forschungen,* 1,5 (Gütersloh, 1929), p. 29.
22. Ibid., p. 31.
23. Ibid., pp. 115f., 41, 43, 109, 117.
24. Ibid., p. 106.
25. Ibid., p. 107f.
26. W. T. Hahn, *Das Mitsterben und Mitauferstehen mit Christus bei Paulus* (Gütersloh, 1937), p. 173.
27. *Appeal to the Churches,* ed. World Council of Churches (Geneva: WCC, 1967).

28. *Des Christen Wehr und Waffen*, p. 29.

29. M. Machovec, *op. cit.*, p. 110.

30. *The Church and the Political Problem of Our Day* (London, 1939), p. 17.

31. *The Epistle to the Philippians* (London, 1962), pp. 101, 106.

32. M. Machovec, *op. cit.*, p. 125.

33. Ibid., p. 113f. E. Busch, in his introduction to *Revolutionary Theology in the Making*, by Karl Barth and Eduard Thurneysen (Richmond: John Knox Press, 1964), p. 14, notes that strict recognition of the supremacy of God and the impossibility of mastering him meant that it was not unconditionally ruled out that this recognition should be complemented by the principle of the autonomy of the secular and a justification of secularization (Gogarten).

34. Hence we have *katalogy* rather than *analogy*.

35. *Church Dogmatics*, III, 1, p. 201.

36. *Collected Works*, vol. I, p. 440. This is not the place, however, to examine more closely the serviceability or range of the concept of analogy, or to ask whether it is a good thing to use Platonism as a mode of expression for theology. It is surely evident that the principle of analogy and Platonism do not overcome the former non-objective view of God's working in the world.

37. *Romans*, p. 313f.

38. Ibid., p. 10, where Barth says that if he has a system it consists in a constant reference both negatively and positively to what Kierkegaard called the infinite qualitative distinction between time and eternity.

39. H. U. von Balthasar, *op. cit.*, pp. 255, 397.

40. G. Wingren, *op. cit.*, p. 37.

41. Ibid., p. 42f.

42. *Collected Works*, vol. I, p. 492.

43. *Op. cit.*, p. 78.

44. Adalbert Huoak, in a review of Machovec's book, *Luth. Monatshefte*, 3 (1964), pp. 170-171.

45. Ibid., p. 171.

46. M. Machovec, *op. cit.*, p. 149.

47. William W. Bartley, *The Retreat to Commitment* (New York, 1962), p. 17. Bartley does not refer specifically to Barth here.

48. H. Zahrnt, *The Question of God: Protestant Theology in the 20th Century* (New York: Harcourt, Brace, & World, 1969), p. 117.

49. E. Bloch, *Atheismus im Christentum*, p. 72.

50. K. Barth, *Protestant Theology in the Nineteenth Century*, p. 645.

51. Ibid., pp. 647, 651.

52. Hermann Kutter, Jr., *Hermann Kutters Lebenswerk* (Zurich, 1965), pp. 131, 126f.
53. *Zeitschrift für Theologie und Kirche*, 56 (1959), p. 265.
54. In *Anfänge der dialektischen Theologie*, vol. I, p. 56f.
55. K. Barth, *The Humanity of God* (London, 1961), p. 55: Theology is objective when without deviating to the right hand or the left it seeks to see, understand, and express the dealings of God with man in which man's dealings with God also arise. On p. 42 he deals with the onesidedness of his earlier theology, stating that this was only one half of the truth.
56. *Church Dogmatics*, IV,3, p. 498.
57. Ibid., pp. 498ff. Cf. the whole of §71 on "The Vocation of Man."
58. Cf. also Barth's self-correction of the "ethico-religious [or religio-social?] Puritanism" which in his earlier period, because of the "dreadful examples" of previous religious eroticism in Mysticism and Pietism had caused him to condemn and strictly forbid speaking of love for God or love for Jesus. This reaction, says Barth, might have had its relative justification, but "we were a little too wise and superior" and also "a little too late with our protest . . . since there was no obvious superfluity of living mystics and pietists of the first rank." The gospel (especially the story of the anointing at Bethany) showed that "without love for God there is no obedience to God or love for one's neighbour" and "without love for Jesus there is no discipleship. Obedience, discipleship and love for one's neighbour arise automatically from this centre" (*Church Dogmatics*, IV,2, pp. 795, 796). The whole passage (pp. 795-798) is well worth reading.
59. K. Barth — E. Thurneysen, *Revolutionary Theology in the Making*, p. 20. That this was always the "sure foundation" for Barth may be seen from statements made at the beginning and at the end of his theological career. In a letter dated November 11, 1918, during a turbulent period, he wrote that if only we had gone back to the Bible earlier we should have had solid ground under our feet (p. 49). Then in 1968, in a discussion with Evangelical Christians from Poland, shortly before his death, he said that ten students who read the Bible played a more important role than a group of demonstrating students (*Informationsbrief der Bekenntnisbewegung "Kein anderes Evangelium,"* no. 19 [May 1969], p. 32).
60. *Church Dogmatics*, IV,2, p. 673f. Barth's theology, too, experienced the truth of what he said about God's care for the Christians (including the theologian!): "The Christian, hemmed in . . . yet not broken nor choked nor perishing nor dying, but living, may emerge again and with good hope for his next steps and steps beyond, and

may enjoy peace and joy, and even great peace and great joy" (*Church Dogmatics*, IV,3, p. 654).

Chapter 4. THE COLLAPSE OF THE DOCTRINE OF GOD: The Vanished God of Atheistic Theology

1. Jonas has shown how the adoption of Heidegger's philosophy in theology necessarily affected the view of activity in this world. He argues that Heidegger's view of thought as man's true calling and his proper answer to the summons of "being" instead of action, neighborly love, resistance to evil, and promotion of the good has come to serve as a model for theology. *Evangelische Theologie*, 24 (1964), p. 635.

2. *The Humanity of God*, p. 42: Barth quotes a line to this extent from German poetry: "And as she warbled, a thousand voices in the field sang it back."

3. At a conference on the Lord's Supper at Arnoldshain/Germany after the Second World War.

4. *Festschrift für G. Dehn*, ed. W. Schneemelcher (Neukirchen, 1957), p. 8.

5. Hans Jonas says that in his view "the crucifixion was rather more than a speech event. Must I tell these Christian theologians this? Apparently so. For I read . . . : 'Our answer to the summons of revelation is in speech.' Is man's answer in speech really what it is all about [in the Bible]? An answer to what? I hear questions to man as the doer of deeds, not the speaker of words: 'Adam where art thou?' 'Cain, where is Abel, thy brother?'" (*op. cit.*, p. 629).

6. *Atheismus im Christentum*, p. 78.

7. S. Kierkegaard, *Training in Christianity* (London, 1944), cf. pp. 245ff.

8. P. Schütz, *Warum ich noch ein Christ bin* [Why I am still a Christian] (Berlin, 1937), pp. 113, 114, 93, 116. The whole book, which has just been reprinted, is important for our theme. It is based on the difficulty a young person has in finding any traces of God today.

9. *Dialogue with Trypho*, p. 3.

10. *Evangelische Theologie*, 26 (1966), p. 671f.

11. *Verkündigung als Information*, vol. I (1968), p. 150. Cf. E. Grässer, "Die falsch programmierte Theologie, Kritische Anmerkungen zu ihrer gegenwärtigen Situation," *Evangelische Kommentare*, 1 (1968), pp. 694-699.

12. "Gibt es ein atheistisches Christentum?" *Merkur*, 23 (Stuttgart, 1969), Heft 249, p. 40.

13. Paul Tillich, *The Courage to Be* (New Haven: Yale University Press, 1952), pp. 182ff.

14. Ibid., p. 184.
15. H. Dee, "Die Vergebung von Sünden," *Evangelische Theologie*, 26 (1966), pp. 540-551; the reference is to p. 547.
16. H. Gollwitzer, "Zu Helmut Dee, 'Vergebung von Sünden,'" ibid., pp. 652-662.
17. P. Van Buren, *The Secular Meaning of the Gospel* (London, 1963), pp. 156, 198. Cf. S. M. Ogden, "The Temporality of God," in *Zeit und Geschichte, Festschrift fü Rudolf Bultmann* (Tübingen, 1964), pp. 395ff. and in analysis E. L. Mascall, *The Secularization of Christianity* (London, 1965), pp. 40-105.
18. *Op. cit.,* pp. 33-44.
19. Ibid., p. 37.
20. Ibid., pp. 38ff.
21. Ibid., p. 39.
22. Ibid., p. 38.
23. Ibid., pp. 39-44; cf. p. 40: " . . . to act like Jesus himself . . . There is no Father."
24. Ibid., p. 41.
25. *Loc. cit.*
26. R. J. Campbell, *The New Theology* (New York, 1907), p. 8.
27. *Theol. Lit. Ztg.* (1912), p. 306.
28. E. Petri, "Zur gegenwärtigen kirchlichen Lage," *Neue kirchliche Zeitschrift*, 20 (Leipzig, 1909), pp. 24-42, esp. 32- 34.
29. *Op. cit.,* p. 306.
30. J. Wendland, *Die neue Diesseitsreligion, Religionsheschichtliche Volksbücher*, V,13 (Tübingen, 1914), pp. 9, 14. On p. 26 he also points out that the idea that "God must be in lovers" is already found in 1800 in Schleiermacher's *Lucinde*.
31. K. Barth, "Concluding Unscientific Postscript on Schleiermacher," pp. 261-279 in his *The Theology of Schleiermacher*, ed. D. Ritschl, trans. Geoffrey W. Bromiley (Grand Rapids: Eerdmans Publishing Co., 1982), p. 271.
32. Cf. Reinhold Niebuhr's *Moral Man and Immoral Society* of 1932 and his *An Interpretation of Christian Ethics* of 1935.
33. This answer, by the way, explains the place that Marxism gives the church in, e.g., the Soviet Union. God and man, church and world, are kept apart. So long as the church does not preach the kingdom of God and the doing of his will on earth as in heaven, it may be tolerated and gradually wither away. Thus the church is compulsorily confined to the cultic sphere. Marxism is convinced that religion will die if it is detached from the earth and left hanging in the air.

34. *Romans*, p. 318.
35. In a letter to Thurneysen, *op. cit.*, p. 43.
36. J. Maritain, *The Peasant of the Garonne* (New York: Holt, Rinehart, & Winston, 1968), p. 12f.
37. *Loc. cit.*

Chapter 5. RECOVERING THE TRUTH: Experiencing the Reality of God in the World

1. A. Schlatter, *Petrus und Paulus* (Stuttgart, 1937), p. 173.
2. *Paulus der Bote Jesu. Eine Deutung seiner Briefe an die Korinther*, 2nd ed. (Stuttgart, 1956), p. 339.
3. Ibid., pp. 337-339.
4. Ibid., p. 338.
5. W. Schweitzer, *Gotteskindschaft, Wiedergeburt und Erneuerung im Neuen Testament und seiner Umwelt*, Diss. (Tübingen, 1943).
6. *Romans*, p. 312.
7. *Glauben und Verstehen*, vol. I, p. 310.
8. E.g. in *KM*, p. 202: "not visible or open to proof."
9. *Theologische Fragen und Antworten. Gesammelte Aufsätze*, vol. III (Zollikon, 1957), p. 22f.
10. "Die Aufweisbarkeit des Heilsgeschehens nach dem Neuen Testament," *Evangelische Theologie*, 11 (1951-52), pp. 484-502; cf. also Schmitz' "Die Wirklichkeit des Heils nach dem Neuen Testament," *Die Furche*, 16 (1930), pp. 2-23, esp. p. 22.
11. *Op. cit.*, pp. 484f., 495, 499, 502.
12. K. Barth, *Protestant Theology in the Nineteenth Century*, p. 640f. Barth himself once took this way of moving from the predicates to the subject, from the "substance" to the "wording of the name"; cf. his instructive essay "Die Wirklichkeit des neuen Menschen," *Theologische Studien*, 27 (Zollikon-Zurich, 1950), esp. p. 13.
13. T. Boman, *Hebrew Thought Compared with Greek* (Philadelphia: Westminster Press, 1960), p. 107.
14. A. Schlatter, *Petrus und Paulus*, p. 35.
15. W. Herrmann, "Die Wirklichkeit Gottes" (1914) in *Schriften zur Grundlegung der Theologie*, vol. II (Munich, 1967), pp. 290-317, esp. pp. 294, 298.
16. *Die Tragweite der Wissenschaft*, vol. I, p. 145.
17. O. Cullmann, *Salvation in History* (London, 1967), pp. 153, 156, 161, 310, 326.
18. *Church Dogmatics*, IV,3, p. 500.
19. Alan Thornhill, *Hide Out* (London: Westminster Publications, 1969), p. 62.

INDEX OF NAMES

LEN

1 - 800
977 2846

July 12th —